on track ...

The Beatles 1962-1966

every album, every song

Alberto Bravin and Andrew Wild

sonicbondpublishing.com

Sonicbond Publishing Limited
www.sonicbondpublishing.co.uk
Email: info@sonicbondpublishing.co.uk

First Published in the United Kingdom 2025
First Published in the United States 2025

British Library Cataloguing in Publication Data:
A Catalogue record for this book is available from the British Library

ISBN 978-1-78952-355-3

Typeset in ITC Garamond Std & ITC Avant Garde Gothic
Printed and bound in England

Graphic design and typesetting: Full Moon Media

Cover author photo: Greg Spawnton

Follow us on social media:
Twitter: https://twitter.com/SonicbondP
Instagram: www.instagram.com/sonicbondpublishing_/
Facebook: www.facebook.com/SonicbondPublishing/

Linktree QR code:

Without going outside his door, one understands all that takes place under the sky; without looking out from his window, one sees the Tao of Heaven. The farther that one goes out from himself, the less he knows. Therefore, the sages got their knowledge without travelling, gave their right names to things without seeing them, and accomplished their ends without any purpose of doing so.
From the 47th chapter of the *Tao Te Ching*, credited to Laozi (400 BCE)

Every new Beatles LP moved things onto a new plane of rhythmic sensuality as if we were all ascending from floor to floor in a transparent building that swayed more as we climbed higher.
From *May Week Was In June: Unreliable Memoirs III* by Clive James (1990)

One of the greatest of The Beatles' achievements was the songwriting juggling act they managed for most of their career. Far from moving sequentially from one genre to another (as is sometimes conveniently suggested), the group maintained in parallel their mastery of the traditional, catchy chart hit while simultaneously forging rock and dabbling with a wide range of peripheral influences from Country to vaudeville. What other artist can span the ultimate extremes of 'All Together Now' and 'Revolution 9'?
From *Songwriting Secrets Of The Beatles* by Dominic Pedler (2003)

Also by Andrew Wild

Books About Music
Pink Floyd Song By Song (Fonthill, 2017)
Queen On Track (Sonicbond, 2018)
The Beatles: An A-Z Guide To Every Song (Sonicbond, 2019)
Solo Beatles 1969-1980 On Track (Sonicbond, 2020)
Crosby, Stills And Nash On Track (Sonicbond, 2020)
Dire Straits On Track (Sonicbond, 2021)
Fleetwood Mac In The 1970s (Sonicbond, 2021)
Eric Clapton Solo On Track (Sonicbond, 2021)
Eric Clapton Sessions (Sonicbond, 2022)
Phil Collins In The 1980s (Sonicbond, 2022)
The Allman Brothers Band On Track (Sonicbond, 2023)
A Mirror Of Dreams: The Progressive Rock Revival 1981-1983 (Kingmaker, 2024)
Live Aid: The Greatest Show On Earth, 13 July 1985 (Sonicbond, 2024)
Four Sides Of The Circle (Rumble Strips, 2024)
The Beautiful South + The Housemartins On Track (Sonicbond, 2025)
A Playground Of Broken Hearts: The Progressive Rock Revival 1984-1989 (Kingmaker, 2025)

Books About Films
James Bond On Screen (Sonicbond, 2022)

Local History
108 Steps Around Macclesfield (Sigma Press, 1994/2nd Edition, Rumble Strips, 2018)
Exploring Chester (Sigma Press, 1996/Re-Publication, Rumble Strips, 2018)
Ever Forward (MADS, 1997)

Biographies
Play On: The Official Biography Of Twelfth Night (Twelfth Night, 2009)
One For The Record: The Official Biography Of Galahad (Avalon, 2013/2nd Edition, 2018)
His Love: The Art, Music And Faith Of Geoff Mann (Sonicbond, 2023)

Books About Comics
The Perfect Marvel Comics Collection – 1939-1985 (Rumble Strips, 2022)

Plays
The Difficult Crossing (Stagescripts, 2016)
A Difficult Man (Rumble Strips, 2021)

As Editor
Stored In Clocks And Mortal Shadows: Geoff Mann's Poems And Lyrics 1973-1993
(Twelfth Night, 2024)

Dedication

Thank you to Nick Jackson and Mark Lewisohn.

To the memories of Beryl Bell and Mario Bravin.

<table>
<tr><th colspan="2">The Authors' Twenty Favourite Beatles Songs</th></tr>
<tr><th>Andy's</th><th>Alberto's</th></tr>
<tr><td>'A Day In The Life'</td><td>'And Your Bird Can Sing'</td></tr>
<tr><td>'Dear Prudence'</td><td>'Being For The Benefit Of Mr. Kite!'</td></tr>
<tr><td colspan="2">'Come Together'</td></tr>
<tr><td></td><td>'Don't Let Me Down'</td></tr>
<tr><td></td><td>'Day Tripper'</td></tr>
<tr><td></td><td>'Drive My Car'</td></tr>
<tr><td></td><td>'Eleanor Rigby'</td></tr>
<tr><td></td><td>'The Fool On The Hill'</td></tr>
<tr><td></td><td>'Girl'</td></tr>
<tr><td colspan="2">'Golden Slumbers-Carry That Weight-The End'</td></tr>
<tr><td>'Here Comes The Sun'</td><td>'Happiness Is A Warm Gun'</td></tr>
<tr><td>'Here, There And Everywhere'</td><td>'In My Life'</td></tr>
<tr><td>'I Am The Walrus'</td><td>'I've Got A Feeling'</td></tr>
<tr><td>'I Saw Her Standing There'</td><td></td></tr>
<tr><td colspan="2">'I Want You (She's So Heavy)</td></tr>
<tr><td>'I'll Be Back'</td><td>'The Long And Winding Road'</td></tr>
<tr><td>'Lucy In The Sky With Diamonds'</td><td>'She's Leaving Home'</td></tr>
<tr><td>'Norwegian Wood (This Bird Has Flown)'</td><td></td></tr>
<tr><td>'Oh! Darling'</td><td></td></tr>
<tr><td>'Rain'</td><td></td></tr>
<tr><td colspan="2">'Something'</td></tr>
<tr><td>'Strawberry Fields Forever</td><td>'While My Guitar Gently Weeps'</td></tr>
<tr><td>'There's A Place'</td><td></td></tr>
<tr><td>'Tomorrow Never Knows'</td><td></td></tr>
<tr><td colspan="2">'Within You Without You'</td></tr>
<tr><td>'The Word'</td><td>'Your Mother Should Know'</td></tr>
</table>

Foreword

My journey into the weird world of music began with (what will become) a familiar melody, a harmony that has accompanied my days since my childhood. The Beatles have not only been a band to me, but a constant companion, a presence that has marked the most significant moments of my life. From the first notes heard from my dad's turntable to the discovery of their stories, their intricate songwriting and 'universal' songs, every note was a revelation capable of igniting my imagination and making me dream.

The Beatles have profoundly influenced my growth, shaping my musical tastes and enriching my vision of the world.

This book is the fruit of the unbreakable bond that I have developed with their music, a tribute to these four lads from Liverpool that has left an indelible mark on my heart.

Alberto Bravin, Trieste, 2025

Like Alberto, I first heard The Beatles from my father. I remember listening to the Red and Blue albums in the mid-seventies when he bought one of those desk-sized hi-fi systems and some records to play on it. I had most of their albums on vinyl as a student – including a vintage 1965 copy of *Rubber Soul*, what happened to that, I wonder – and remember buying all of the CD reissues in 1987-1988.

And then, in about 1993, I placed a small ad in *Q* or *Mojo*, looking for a copy of *The Beatles At The Hollywood Bowl*. A local guy answered and, as part of the deal, he gave (or perhaps sold) me a cassette of several unreleased versions of 'Strawberry Fields Forever' and the session outtakes for 'Misery'. These must have been copies of the *Unsurpassed Masters* bootlegs.

It seemed that there were other live and studio recordings in circulation. I collected them all. This took 25 years. And, in doing so, I gained a new appreciation of those original albums and singles from the 1960s and it's those that we celebrate in this book.

Andrew Wild, Rainow, 2025

Preface

Other than 'I Me Mine' and some minor overdubs, The Beatles' entire EMI/ Apple catalogue was recorded in fewer than seven years: from 4 September 1962 through to 20 August 1969. Twelve albums, twenty-two singles, two standalone EPs, 211 songs.

That in itself is remarkable enough.

However, the quality of the music, the rapid development of musical complexity, and the innovations in studio production lifted The Beatles above every other band. It's impossible to disagree with this statement and if you try, then you're simply wrong.

Sometimes, in lesser inspired on-line clickbait, you'll see lazy articles such as 'The 10 Worst Beatles Songs Of All Time'. These always seem to include the likes of 'Maggie Mae', 'Wild Honey Pie', 'Rocky Raccoon' and 'Revolution 9'. And, elsewhere, there will be endless 'best of' lists which are, obviously, subjective. See below.

It's not unusual for the same song to appear on both 'best' and 'worst' lists: 'Within You Without You', or 'I Want You (She's So Heavy)' or even 'Here Comes The Sun'. One writer, who we won't name and shame here, described 'Yesterday' as 'a sickly, mawkish, ubiquitous, unflushable turd' and writes that 'I Want You (She's So Heavy') 'alternates between a turgid descending riff that should never have made it past soundcheck, and the most coma-inducing of blues jams. When it finally wraps up, a full eight minutes later, you'll snap back to consciousness to find you've drooled down your front.'

We disagree, of course.

True, the Fab Four were not always fab. But that some writers take the time and expend energy to point this out and purposefully dismiss perfect songs such as 'Yesterday' merely serves to remind us that, most of the time, The Beatles were unarguably brilliant.

And then we have the 'boy band' theory ('they are the Backstreet Boys of the early 60s who decided to do drugs and become artists' – wrong) or that Ringo was a bad drummer (very wrong). Oh, and Paul's very definitely not dead.

From a technical point of view, for much of the period covered in this book, The Beatles worked on two-track and four-track recording technology under extreme time pressures. They had to push themselves to be inventive in the time allocated. And, despite these restrictions, or perhaps because of them, they wrote and recorded songs which are still revered. They were the best band in the 1960s, without question.

We've listened to, digested and discussed the entire Beatles back catalogue to remind us why we love their music. It opened our eyes and our ears once again and took us back to why we are still so emotionally invested in this music from sixty or more years ago. Why are these songs still relevant? How do they affect us today?

Answer: they were bloody good. They still are.

on track ...

The Beatles

1962-1966

Contents

Introduction

The Beatles' story has been told many times. Even now, it still seems utterly unbelievable.

It begins in 1956. The impact of Elvis Presley's on global pop music cannot be underestimated. It was like Presley, just turning 21 when his first RCA single was released and irreparably charismatic, had somehow been beamed down from space.

'Heartbreak Hotel' was released as the year began, on 27 January. Four months later it had crossed the Atlantic, appearing on the UK charts at number 15 on 17 May 1956. As that song began its climb up the 'hit parade', five places below was another called 'Rock Island Line' by Scottish-born singer Lonnie Donegan. Donegan can lay claim to inventing 'skiffle', a low-budget spin-off from the British post-war jazz scene. Skiffle allowed almost beginners to sing American folk and blues songs with cheap instruments and three chords.

'Rock Island Line' took over eighteen months to gain traction: it was recorded in July 1954 and burned slowly. In the meantime, rock 'n' roll – amplified, up-tempo blues music – began to take hold. Pioneers such as Chuck Berry, Little Richard, Fats Domino and Carl Perkins had their first hits in 1955 with 'Maybelline', 'Tutti Frutti', 'Ain't That A Shame' and 'Blue Suede Shoes'. Elvis Presley, who took white country and western and added a black attitude and beat, signed for RCA in 1955, and recorded his first single for them early the following year.

'Heartbreak Hotel' is dark, echoing, sexy and utterly original. It stayed on the UK charts until the week before the sixteenth birthday of one John Lennon of Liverpool. Lennon had a problematic childhood but was a bright kid, attending grammar school and excelling at art and causing trouble.

Lennon borrowed a guitar, learned a few chords from his vivacious mother Julia and formed a skiffle group with some school pals which he named The Quarrymen after their school, Quarry Bank. They picked up local gigs whenever they could.

At one of these, during a church fete in Woolton on 6 July 1957, Lennon was introduced by a mutual friend to another aspiring musician: the just-turned-fifteen James Paul McCartney. As Paul told *Record Collector* in 1995, 'I remember John singing a song called 'Come Go With Me.' He'd heard it on the radio. He didn't really know the verses, but he knew the chorus. The rest he just made up himself. I just thought, 'Well, he looks good, he's singing well and he seems like a great lead singer to me.' Of course, he had his glasses off, so he really looked suave. I remember John was good.'

Lennon's and McCartney's paths had crossed previously. Beatles historian Mark Lewisohn suggests that they met, and spoke, outside the shop where Paul did his paper round. This is at 85 Woolton Road, five minutes bike ride from Paul's home. This cannot be proven for certain, but perhaps explains how Paul was able to summon up the courage to play guitar and sing in front of the older boy at the Woolton Fete. Paul: 'My memory of meeting John for the first time is very clear. I can still see John now – checked shirt and slightly curly hair. I remember thinking, 'I wouldn't mind being in a group with him."

It's difficult to think of a less likely location for a world-changing event than a suburban church hall, but that's where Paul McCartney auditioned for The Quarrymen that afternoon. Lennon was impressed by Paul's ability to play the tricky 'Twenty Flight Rock' by Eddie Cochran and his uncanny knack for singing like one of their shared idols, Little Richard.

John and his best mate Pete Shotton talked about whether to ask Paul to join The Quarry Men. A couple of weeks later Shotton saw Paul riding his bike in Woolton and asked him to join. Their partnership would last just over twelve years, but John Lennon and Paul McCartney together changed the face of popular music.

Paul's first gig with The Quarrymen was on 18 October 1957 at the New Clubmoor Hall in the Norris Green area of Liverpool. Recalling later, Paul said:

> When I got up on stage at the very first gig, I totally blew it. I had never experienced these things called nerves before … I was playing 'Guitar Boogie' and I knew it fine off-stage… but on stage, my fingers all went very stiff and then found themselves underneath the strings instead of on top of them. So I vowed that night that it was the end of my career as the lead guitar player. I just thought I'll lean back. So me and John kind of both did that around that same time; both became rhythm guitarists.

Their lead guitarist wasn't too far away, though. George Harrison attended the same school as Paul McCartney, Liverpool Institute High School. George was in the year below Paul (he was nine months younger – he always was 9 months younger than Paul) and they would often share the same bus ride to and from school, talking music and playing guitars. In February 1958, Paul invited George, then aged fifteen, to watch The Quarrymen. George auditioned, and impressed John with his playing, but the band's leader thought that Harrison was too young. After a month's persistence, and during a second meeting arranged by Paul, George legendarily played 'Raunchy' on the upper deck of a Liverpool bus. The Quarrymen enlisted George Harrison as lead guitarist. A few months later, on 14 July, they recorded two songs at a small studio in Liverpool. 'That'll Be The Day' has the unmistakable twang of John Lennon's lead vocals. Remarkably, 'In Spite Of All The Danger' was a McCartney original (co-credited to Harrison because he wrote the guitar solo). Even at this early stage, The Quarrymen were keen to write and record their own material.

By January 1959, Lennon's Quarry Bank friends had left the group, and he began his studies at the Liverpool College Of Art, conveniently located adjacent to the Liverpool Institute High School. It is during this period that

John, Paul and George became firm friends. They would play together on their lunch breaks and at each other's family homes. Gigs were few.

John Lennon's closest friend at art school was a talented artist called Stuart Sutcliffe. One of his works, *Summer Painting*, was exhibited at the second Biennial John Moores Exhibition at the Walker Art Gallery in Liverpool between November 1959 and January 1960. John Moores was a local businessman and philanthropist and bought Sutcliffe's painting for £65 (the equivalent of £1,800 in 2025).

'So what do you do with £65?' McCartney mused in *The Beatles Anthology*. 'We all reminded him over a coffee: 'Funny you should have got that amount, Stuart – it is very near the cost of a Hofner bass.' He said, 'No, I can't just spend all that.' It was a fortune in those days, like an inheritance. He said he had to buy canvases or paint. We said, 'Stu, see reason, love. A Hofner, a big ace group ... fame!' He gave in and bought this big Hofner bass that dwarfed him. The trouble was he couldn't play well. This was a bit of a drawback, but it looked good, so it wasn't too much of a problem.'

Sutcliffe, despite his limitations as a bass player, would have a huge influence on the way that the band presented themselves. The first was to provide a new name. The trio of Lennon, McCartney and Harrison had been styling themselves at various times as Johnny And The Moondogs, The Rainbows, Japage 3 and even their old Quarrymen moniker.

Stuart Sutcliffe suggested changing the band's name to Beatals, as a tribute to Buddy Holly And The Crickets. The name would vary throughout the first half of 1960. By the summer, they had settled on The Beatles.

One of the characters in their orbit was a Scouse chancer called Allan Williams, owner of the band's preferred hangout, The Jacaranda, close to the Institute and Art College. Williams had fingers in many pies. As well as acting as The Beatles' booking agent, he also had an acquaintanceship with the promoter Larry Parnes. Parnes had a 'stable' of interchangeable solo singers with unlikely stage names and needed a backing band for a seven-date Scottish tour by one of his lesser talents, Johnny Gentle. The Beatles were second, or perhaps third, choice, but they were available should they recruit a drummer. Local musician Tommy Moore, ten years older than the others, undertook the tour but left, bruised and bitter, on their return.

Williams – through a bizarre set of co-incidences – booked The Beatles for a long residency at the Indra Club in Hamburg. This required the rapid recruitment of a permanent drummer. Enter Pete Best, the son of the irrepressible Mona Best, owner of the Casbah Coffee Club, located in the cellar of the family home.

With Best on board, The-name-now-set-in-stone-Beatles and their retinue drove to Hamburg. From 17 August to 21 November, they would perform four hours each night, seven days a week.

'We had to play for hours and hours on end,' Lennon said. 'Every song lasted twenty minutes and had twenty solos in it. That's what improved the playing. There was nobody to copy from. We played what we liked best and the Germans liked it as long as it was loud.'

Here, they met Astrid Kirchherr, Klaus Voormann and Jürgen Vollmer – three young Germans who would have a profound influence on the band's early look. Kirchherr would take the first semi-professional photos of The Beatles: an invaluable record of their time in Hamburg as a five-piece.

Williams booked other Liverpool bands into Hamburg clubs, including Rory Storm And The Hurricanes, who had a very good drummer, in the shape of Richard 'Ringo' Starkey. Another talented British musician, the highly-regarded Tony Sheridan, was also resident, performing American r&b to young fans.

The Beatles' first trip to Hamburg ended in disarray. George Harrison was deported in late November – he wasn't yet eighteen and therefore too young to enter the clubs they were playing – and a week later, Paul McCartney and Pete Best were arrested for alleged arson and were also deported after several hours in police custody. John Lennon returned to Liverpool in early December, while Stu Sutcliffe remained in Hamburg for several weeks having become engaged to Astrid Kirchherr.

Early in 1961, another milestone was passed with the band's first performance at The Cavern Club.

'[The Beatles] were different and they were very well rehearsed because they had come back from three months of torture in Hamburg,' the club's owner Ray McFall told Spencer Leigh. 'The other groups were like Cliff Richard And The Shadows, but The Beatles' music was so vibrant…'

The Beatles returned to Hamburg between 27 March and 2 July 1961, performing at the Top Ten Club. During this second engagement, Astrid Kirchherr cut Stuart Sutcliffe's hair in the 'exi' (existentialist) style, quickly adopted first by George (always the band's snappiest dresser), John and Paul. It was here that they started to wear the leather suits that made them stand out. John also bought a 1958 Rickenbacker 325 Capri guitar.

Stu Sutcliffe left the band during this run of bookings to resume his art studies in Hamburg. Paul McCartney took over on bass, buying a lightweight Höfner 500/1 model. 'I found a nice little shop in the centre of Hamburg,' Paul told *Music Radar* in 1994. 'And I saw this bass in the window, this violin-shaped Höfner. It was a good price, because my dad had always said I shouldn't do the never-never, but we were earning reasonable money. I liked the Höfner's lightness, too. So I bought it, and I think it was only about 30 quid.'

Priced at 287 Deutsche Marks, it was custom made for left-handed Paul. Three more crucial components were in place: the haircuts, distinctive violin bass and the four-piece lineup.

At this time, German bandleader and producer Bert Kaempfert signed The Beatles to a year-long contract with Polydor. Seven titles would be recorded as Tony Sheridan's backing band in one day, possibly two, in the third week of June 1961. One of these, 'Ain't She Sweet' featured throaty lead vocals by

John Lennon. Released as a single in the wake of the band's initial success, 'Ain't She Sweet' reached the top 30 in the UK and number 19 in the US.

A second, an instrumental called 'Beatle Bop', was the first commercially available Beatles' original. Retitled 'Cry For A Shadow', it's initial availability was on a French EP.

They returned to Liverpool as a power-house beat group performing most nights of the weeks in and around Liverpool, as well as building a fan base at The Cavern.

The single 'My Bonnie' was released in October 1961, credited to Tony Sheridan & The Beat Brothers. It reached number 32 on the *Musikmarkt* chart. In due course, this song would lead to another piece in the jigsaw: Brain Epstein.

Epstein ran the record department at his family's Liverpool furniture store and wrote a column in the city's music paper, *Mersey Beat*. The actual truth of why Epstein strolled the two minutes from his shop to the club on 9 November 1961 may never be wholly pinned down. The accepted story is that he first heard of the band when a customer entered his shop asking for a copy of 'My Bonnie'. Stu Sutcliffe had sent a copy to George Harrison, which found its way to the Cavern Club's DJ Bob Wooler. This single copy was played at various venues across Liverpool, generating interest in fans who wanted to buy their own copy. Epstein prided himself in stocking (or being able to acquire) any single – 'My Bonnie' had not been released in the UK, therefore his interest was piqued.

This aspect of how Brian Epstein met The Beatles is part of the story, but not the whole story. NEMS stocked *Mersey Beat* and it's impossible to believe that Brian didn't at least leaf through it. As Paul McCartney later said, 'Brian knew perfectly well who The Beatles were; they were on the front page of the second issue of *Mersey Beat*.'

Nevertheless, that lunchtime visit to The Cavern Club would be crucial both for Epstein and his soon-to-be clients. In his memoirs, written just three years later, Epstein wrote: 'I immediately liked what I heard. They were fresh, and they were honest, and they had what I thought was a sort of presence. I was ... struck by their music, their beat and their sense of humour on stage – and, even afterwards, when I met them, I was struck again by their personal charm. And it was there that, really, it all started.'

Epstein had always been restless, constrained by what he felt were the narrow parameters of the family business. He was looking for something new. He also probably fancied them. A few days later, he offered to manage The Beatles, they accepted and for the next six years, Epstein was utterly devoted to 'the boys'.

Now, everything started to move quickly. The day after the first Epstein-Beatles meeting, the band headlined the first Operation Big Beat at the Tower Ballroom in New Brighton. This five-and-a-half-hour event featured The Beatles, Rory Storm And The Hurricanes (with Ringo on drums), Gerry And

The Pacemakers, The Remo Four and Kingsize Taylor And The Dominoes. The Beatles, as headliners, performed two sets, the first at 8pm and the second at 11.30pm. In between, they headed through the Mersey Tunnel for a separate booking in Knotty Ash. By now, The Beatles were the most popular band in Liverpool.

As 1961 moved into 1962, The Beatles travelled to London for an audition with Decca Records. This was blighted by the band's nerves, thin-sounding equipment, a flawed selection of songs and a long, chilly drive from Liverpool. Decca was not interested. Epstein booked the band into a third residency in Hamburg, to start on 13 April 1962. They arrived to learn of the death of their friend Stuart Sutcliffe.

The Beatles returned to Liverpool after their booking ended on 31 May 1962 and a week later they made their first trip to a soon-to-be-legendary British recording studio. The Beatles were about to record for George Martin, the head of Parlophone, at the EMI Studios in Abbey Road.

1962

'Love Me Do' b/w **'P.S. I Love You'** (Single)

UK single: 5 October 1962. US single: 27 April 1964.
Chart positions. UK: 17. US: 1.

Mark Lewisohn's masterful *Tune In* describes in detail the exhilarating story of how The Beatles were awarded their Parlophone recording contract. That they insisted on 'Love Me Do' as their debut single proved that these four young men were as strong-willed as they were talented. If we imagine the claustrophobic gigs in The Cavern, the wild nights in Hamburg, or the pandemonium of the New Brighton Tower Ballroom, then 'Love Me Do' is totally uncharacteristic.

And yet, decades later, 'Love Mo Do' still sounds fresh and original. Here was the first chapter of The Beatles' Manifesto.

'Love Me Do' (Lennon/McCartney)

Recorded 4 September 1962. Paul McCartney – vocals, bass; John Lennon – vocals, acoustic guitar, harmonica; George Harrison – acoustic rhythm guitar; Ringo Starr – drums.

> Johnny was a schoolboy when he heard his first Beatles song.
> 'Love Me Do' I think it was...
> Bad Company, 'Shooting Star' (1975)

For the most part, 'Love Me Do' gently swings on just two chords: tight and deep in the groove.

'Love Me Do' is original and idiosyncratic. It has a bluesy bridge section (but no seventh chords), bright harmonica and peerless vocals with unusual harmonies – witness the still exhilarating 'pleeeeeease' first heard between 0.23 and 0.27. As Dominic Pedler observes in his book *The Songwriting Secrets Of The Beatles,* 'vocal harmony was the main way in which interest was added to a Beatles arrangement, before exotic instrumentation and studio effects were to bring their own distractions.'

The harmonica riff – borrowed from Bruce Channel's 'Hey! Baby' and Frank Ifield's 'I Remember You', both hits earlier in 1962 – is an example of an unusual and memorable hook or a moment; a harmony or a sound that made listeners prick up their ears to the music of The Beatles.

Ringo Starr had been a member of The Beatles for two and a half weeks when 'Love Me Do' was recorded. If we compare this version with the earlier session with Pete Best (6 June 1962) it's very clear that, in Ringo, they had found a perfect fit. Ringo's simplicity, and the fact that he always played what was exactly right and nothing more has often been maligned over the years. He remains one of the most distinctively musical drummers. He always served the song, didn't showboat and was integral to the sound of The Beatles' music. Anyone who disagrees can speak to us after school.

But what's most important about 'Love Me Do' isn't the composition, the performance or the arrangement – it's that 'Love Me Do' was written and performed by a British vocal/instrumental group. In 1962, these groups simply did not exist. The Beatles broke the mould with their first single.

As 1962 moved into 1963, with 'Love Me Do' at its chart peak of 17, The Beatles were resident mid-table in a top fifty dominated by solo singers (thirty-four different artists) and instrumental acts (nine). There were four American vocal groups – The Four Seasons, The Crystals, The Everly Brothers and The Orlons – and just one British vocal group, The Springfields. This is why 'Love Me Do' was a hit then and remains dazzling today. There was nothing else like it then, and there's nothing like it now.

'P.S. I Love You' (Lennon/McCartney)
Recorded 11 September 1962. Paul McCartney – lead vocals, bass; John Lennon – acoustic guitar, backing vocals; George Harrison – acoustic guitar, backing vocals; Ringo Starr – maracas; Andy White – drums.

On the single version of 'Love Me Do' it's Ringo on the drums. A second recording, a week later, involved session drummer Andy White. It's the 11 September 1962 version which was included on the *Please Please Me* album. 'P.S. I Love You' was recorded in the same sessions as the second version of 'Love Me Do', therefore, White is once more behind the kit.

'P.S. I Love You' was written in Hamburg by a self-taught 20-year old. With a sentimental, epistolatory lyric, unusually rich chord changes, Latin-influenced arrangement (it just needs a 'cha-cha-cha' ending) and brilliantly arranged harmony vocals, it could only have been written by Paul, who is particularly confident in his vocal delivery.

McCartney, even in 1962, makes it all look and sound so easy. This hides a remarkable gift and an enviable talent for songwriting, melody and harmony that marks him out as one of the greatest song-writers of his generation. Not so long before, as the often-repeated story goes, Paul travelled to the other side of Liverpool to meet a guy who knew a B7 chord.

> We used to travel miles for a new chord in Liverpool. We'd take bus rides for hours to visit the guy who knew B7! None of us knew how to finger it and he was the guru. We sat there and he played it a few times; then we all said: 'Brilliant, thanks!' We already had E and A. The B7 chord was the final piece in the jigsaw.
> *Guitar Player*, 1990

McCartney's first-recorded original song, 'In Spite Of All The Danger' uses this exact chord. Four years later, 'P.S. I Love You' has jazzy changes which move through C#7, Bm and Bb to an unusual drop to Em ('I'll be coming *home* again'). It was almost as though McCartney wanted to pack lots of musical colour into the composition.

The Beatles were always impeccable with vocal arrangements. The backing vocals on 'P.S. I Love You' are warm and they change arrangement as the track progresses. Best of all, the three vocalists each get a solo in the second bridge: the first, after 'as I write this letter', is John's impassioned 'oh', then Paul scats 'you know I want you to remember' and finally, George gives us a knowing 'yeah'.

The inclusion of a slow, complex song as the B-side to 'Love Me Do' must have surprised their rocker fans in Liverpool. But then, The Beatles never conformed to expectations.

1963

'Please Please Me' b/w **'Ask My Why'** (Single)

UK single: 11 January 1963. US single: 25 February 1963.
Chart positions. UK: 2. US: did not chart.

The Beatles' first number one single? Well, yes, in every chart apart from the one used historically to record chart positions. But this is the early stirring of the Beatlemania phase in 1963-1964: a killer pairing of two great (and very different) songs which state, unequivocally, 'here we are'…

'Please Please Me' (Lennon/McCartney)

Recorded 26 November 1962. John Lennon – lead vocals, rhythm guitar, harmonica; Paul McCartney – bass, backing vocals; George Harrison – lead guitar, backing vocals; Ringo Starr – drums.

'Please Please Me', unlike 'Love Me Do', exhibits most of The Beatles' early trademarks: tight singing with rich and unusual harmonies, call-and-response vocals, a jump to falsetto ('to reason with *you*'), clever but commercial chord changes (especially under the second word of 'please *please* me'), a hard ending (no fade out) and a strong rock beat, including some classic Ringo drum fills. This was a long way from the formulaic pop of the day. The harmonica introduction looks back to the band's debut single as well as forward to 'From Me To You'. It's exuberant, full of life and 100% John Lennon. Lennon was famously influenced by Roy Orbison, as well as by Bing Crosby's 1930s song 'Please'.

Lennon told *Playboy's* David Sheff in 1980.

> 'Please Please Me' is my song completely,' . 'It was my attempt at writing a Roy Orbison song, would you believe it? I wrote it in the bedroom in my house at Menlove Avenue, which was my auntie's place. I remember the day and the pink coverlet on the bed, and I heard Roy Orbison doing 'Only The Lonely' or something. That's where that came from. And also, I was always intrigued by the words of 'Please, lend me your little ears to my pleas' – a Bing Crosby song. I was always intrigued by the double use of the word 'please'. So, it was a combination of Bing Crosby and Roy Orbison.

Originally recorded in a much slower arrangement, 'Please Please Me' bursts from the traps with energy and brio. They had to get it right: George Martin wanted them to release their earlier recording of the breezy 'How Do You Do It?' and they most certainly did not.

With typical good fortune, much of the UK population was snowed-in at home on 19 January to watch The Beatles perform 'Please Please Me' at the bottom of a seven-act bill on the Saturday night TV show, *Thank Your Lucky Stars*. The programme had been recorded a few days beforehand at Alpha Television Studios in Birmingham squeezed between live bookings in Chatham (12 January) and Ellesmere Port (14 January).

'Please Please Me' also sounded great on the radio. It first registered on the singles chart on 17 January, entering the top twenty by the end of the month. George Martin duly instructed the band to come to EMI to record their first album. 'Please Please Me' spent two months in the top five and was listed as a number one by *New Musical Express* and *Melody Maker,* amongst others. In *Record Retailer*, used to compile official chart statistics, 'Please Please Me' was lodged behind Frank Ifield's 'Wayward Wind' for one week and Cliff Richard's 'Summer Holiday' for another.

Things were about to change. The Beatles had arrived.

Meanwhile, 'How Do You Do It?' was recorded for EMI by Gerry And The Pacemakers on 22 January 1963 and, as producer George Martin predicted, it was a number one hit. The Beatles' very lacklustre version is on *Anthology 1*.

'Ask Me Why' (Lennon/McCartney)

Recorded 26 November 1962. John Lennon – vocals, acoustic guitar; Paul McCartney – bass, backing vocals; George Harrison – lead guitar, backing vocals; Ringo Starr – drums.

'Ask Me Why' is a classic B-side which pairs an uneven Latin-influenced beat with a carefully arranged three-part vocal harmony that drops out to expose Lennon's magnificent lead vocal breaking on 'cry'.

They also borrow from The Miracles. The opening guitar lick is very obviously adapted from their 1961 song 'What's So Good About Goodbye'. The ending adds another twist. 'The listener can only swoon,' fawns Dominic Pedler, 'as a delicately unfolding G#m7 (at 2.17) leaves us with the softest of jazz lullaby endings.'

'Ask Me Why' was recorded in just six takes: it had been in their live set for around half a year by then. They had been pleased enough with the song to record it for the BBC in June 1962 (the arrangement was in place five months ahead of the formal recording session, if taken at a brighter clip) and subsequently played a phenomenal live version at their last Hamburg show on 31 December 1962.

Please Please Me (UK album)

22 March 1963.

Chart position. UK: 1.

The Beatles' carefully presented image – on the face of it, they were four identikit musicians who were difficult to tell apart – disguised four road-hardened and experienced musicians. At 21, 21, 20 and 19 years they had probably logged more stage hours than *any other* band in the UK when they entered EMI Studios in Abbey Road to record ten songs for their debut album *in a single day*. It was brilliantly recorded with shimmering guitars, pounding bass (mixed low until the 1987 CD version), Ringo's masterful drumming and startling vocals.

As first albums go, *Please Please Me* isn't flawless. But as a vehicle for showcasing The Beatles' strong performance and composition skills, and in presenting their individual personalities, it remains a superb achievement for a young band with limited studio experience.

Simon Philo in *British Invasion: The Crosscurrents Of Musical Influence* (2014) suggests, '*Please Please Me…* marked the dawning of the age of the self-sufficient pop group, whose members would generate most, if not all, of their own material, and therefore represented the first of a number of key moments peppering The Beatles' life span that would inspire others to actively create rather than passively consume.'

Or, put more simply: one, two, three, faw!

'I Saw Her Standing There' (Lennon/McCartney)

Recorded 11 February 1963. Paul McCartney – lead vocals, bass, hand claps; John Lennon – rhythm guitar, backing vocals, hand claps; George Harrison – lead guitar, hand claps; Ringo Starr – drums, hand claps.

'I Saw Her Standing There' is like a slap in the face. It's surely a candidate for the best-ever opening song on a debut album.

McCartney, as principal songwriter, cops the changes from 'The Saints Go Marching In', recorded with Tony Sheridan in Hamburg in 1961, and adds the bass line from Chuck Berry's 'I'm Talking About You' and the rhythm guitar from Arthur Alexander's 'A Shot Of Rhythm And Blues'. And although the verses follow standard I-IV-V rock and roll changes, McCartney adds one thrilling chord change at the end of each verse as a supercharged Am (guitars) is underpinned with a C (bass) and harmonised 'wooh', first heard at 0.25.

Dominic Pedler suggests that 'it's [a] devious… chord… that transforms the song from a frivolous r&b standard into a pop classic while turning, as one writer [Tim Riley in *Tell Me Why*] suggests 'implied innocence into sexual bravado'. It's Amazing, really, what one chord can do.'

Like most of their first album, 'I Saw Her Standing There' is a song about sex that is disguised as a song about love. The Beatles know this: their fans know this. They were young, yes, but hardly naive after five residencies in Hamburg. The shuffling 'Well my heart went boom' bridge has a palpable sexual tension as it builds to 'I held her hand in mine' and a climatic, almost orgasmic release as we fall back into the verse.

It's also a great group performance. John's rhythm guitar and Paul's bass and vocals drive the track. George's solo is tight and fluent and Ringo is, as ever, perfect, especially when he adds his trademark fills between the different sections with sharp, syncopated snare raps at 0.20, 0.44, 1.11, 1.22, 1.35, 1.57, 2.13, 2.25 and 2.42.

Listen closely at 1.30 when John messes up the words, singing 'when' instead of 'since' and laughs through the next phrase.

The original stereo mix, with the vocals on the right and rhythm track on the left, sounds very odd to modern ears. Giles Martin's 2023 remix adds width and body with guitars in either channel and pushes forward the bass and drums. It sounds terrific on Spotify, which is perhaps why it exists.

We prefer the punchy mono from the original album.

'Misery' (Lennon/McCartney)

Recorded 11 and 20 February 1963. John Lennon – lead vocals, acoustic guitar; Paul McCartney – lead vocals, bass; George Harrison – lead guitar; Ringo Starr – drums; George Martin – piano.

'Misery' was written for Helen Shapiro, with whom The Beatles were touring in late January 1963. Work started as they were backstage in Stoke-on-Trent and was later finished in Liverpool.

Without overthinking it, 'Misery' is one of two songs on *Please Please Me* that hint at an inward-looking unhappiness, a touch of lovelorn depression. Both 'There's A Place' and 'Misery' portray the flip side of relationships, the conflicting emotions... the downs as well as the ups. It's no co-incidence that 'Ask Me Why' also uses the word 'misery'.

Like 'Do You Want To Know A Secret?' and, in fact, 'My Bonnie', 'Misery' starts with a slow, dramatic semi-spoken introduction. Paul and John sing in unison, mostly, but there are some lovely harmonies at the end of certain lines, especially on the word 'misery'. Macca also uses that odd 'shh' sound in 'shend', and John pops in a bit of Del Shannon falsetto in a coda.

Outtakes confirm that George Martin's piano was a later addition. Take 2 breaks down when Martin complains that George Harrisons was using too much treble; takes 4 and 5 stutter to a halt when Lennon sings the wrong words. Ringo's drum fills and George's guitar flourishes are removed after take 6, the band and/or producer seemingly preferring simplicity in this case.

Shapiro turned the song down – the lyrics are very downbeat for a 16-year-old – but fellow tour member Kenny Lynch recorded it himself, becoming the first performer to cover a Lennon-McCartney song, and even then, he modified the lyrics slightly.

The placing of the song immediately after 'I Saw Her Standing There' – a slow, introspective song after a brash, up-tempo opening – suggests that producer George Martin laid out the album as though he was plotting a live concert. His original idea of recording the band at The Cavern is given some life in the sequencing of *Please Please Me*.

'Anna (Go To Him)' (Alexander)

Recorded 11 February 1963. John Lennon – vocals, acoustic guitar; Paul McCartney – bass, backing vocals; George Harrison – lead guitar, backing vocals; Ringo Starr – drums.

Here is the first of The Beatles recorded cover versions. The thousands of hours and hundreds of songs from their long days and nights on the Hamburg and Liverpool club circuit enabled The Beatles not only to assimilate other artists' songs, but to arrange them for two guitars, bass and drums. George replicates Floyd Cramer's distinctive piano phrases from the original, Ringo negotiates the loping rhythm and the arrangement of the backing vocals is impeccable.

'Anna (Go To Him') was released as a single by Arthur Alexander in September 1962, and was a particular favourite of John Lennon, as he told *Melody Maker* in February 1963:

> We don't play real rhythm and blues ... Our musical tastes are various – we like a little bit of classical music, a bit of modern jazz, a bit of everything ... One artist I like is Arthur Alexander – you don't hear much of him over here.

There are versions of three other Alexander songs on the Star-Club recordings which pre-date the *Please Please Me* sessions by only six weeks.

There is a weary regret in Lennon's vocals in the verses. This switches to a full-throated, anguished pleading in 'all of my life I've been searching for a girl' and 'what am I supposed to do?' in the chorus. The band then drop right back down into the next verse with a dynamic, goosebumps-inducing dip in volume. Lennon's voice had an occasional nasal quality, and his heavy cold is very obvious on 'go with him' at the end of each verse.

If you think 'Anna (Go To Him)' is good, then a scintillating version of Arthur Alexander's 'Soldier Of Love' can be heard on *Live At The BBC*.

'Chains' (Goffin/King)

Recorded 11 February 1963. George Harrison – lead vocals, lead guitar; John Lennon – rhythm guitar, harmonica, backing vocals; Paul McCartney – bass, backing vocals; Ringo Starr – drums.

Part of The Beatles' appeal – not so obvious in early 1963, perhaps, but crucial as they broke internationally – was their four distinct personalities and four very different voices. Here, we have George on lead vocals for a cover of a song written by Carole King and Gerry Goffin. It was first recorded by The Cookies, a New York vocal group who sang back-up on 'The Locomotion' by Little Eva and Neil Sedaka's 'Breaking Up Is Hard To Do'.

The Beatles speed along their version, replacing the saxophone in the original with reverbed harmonica. They were keen on the song, perhaps because it gave George a vocal spotlight, and recorded it four times for BBC radio.

'Boys' (Dixon/Farrell)

Recorded 11 February 1963. Ringo Starr – vocals, drums; John Lennon – rhythm guitar, backing vocals; Paul McCartney – bass, backing vocals; George Harrison – lead guitar, backing vocals.

Originally by The Shirelles, the B-side of their hit single 'Will You Love Me Tomorrow' (UK no. 4, March 1961), this is Ringo's vocal spot on *Please Please Me*. He had sung the song in his time as a member of Rory Storm And The

Hurricanes. Pete Best was featured vocalist for The Beatles' own performances prior to 1962 and recorded his own (pretty decent) version in 1965.

It's a simple twelve-bar rock and roll song recorded live in one take, confirming The Beatles' prowess as a tight unit, especially as they rave on in the last third and threaten to get out of control. Macca whoops through George's perfunctory guitar solo which has none of the pizzazz of King Curtis' saxophone on the original. Ringo's vocals are best described as enthusiastic, quite different to the sensual purr of Shirley Owens in The Cookies' recording.

It's the same four guys, but Ringo's spotlight always added colour to their albums and live shows.

'Ask Me Why'
Previously released as a single.

'Please Please Me'
Previously released as a single.

'Love Me Do'
Recorded 11 September 1962. Paul McCartney – vocals, bass; John Lennon – vocals, acoustic guitar, harmonica; George Harrison – acoustic rhythm guitar; Ringo Starr – tambourine; Andy White – drums.
The album version of 'Love Me Do' is identical to the single take recorded one week earlier, but with one key difference. The drums are by session player Andy White who copies Ringo's arrangement beat for beat but plays the song ever so slightly faster – the album version is about two seconds shorter.

'P.S. I Love You'
Previously released as a single.

'Baby It's You' (David/Williams/Bacharach)
Recorded 11 and 20 February 1963. John Lennon – vocals, rhythm guitar; Paul McCartney – bass, backing vocals; George Harrison – lead guitar, backing vocals; Ringo Starr – drums; George Martin – celesta.
Part of The Beatles' live set for three years, 'Baby It's You' is a cover of a song by The Shirelles, like 'Boys'. It was recorded in three takes in the third and final session of 11 February 1963, the ninth song of the day. The strain on Lennon's voice is starting to show. His voice starts to break on 'don't want nobody' at 2.16. 'Twist And Shout' would be recorded immediately after this. His vocal performance is much more aggressive than the more soulful, sassy original.

George Martin added celesta, a bell-like cousin of the piano, in a later overdub. This is more palatable than the fairground organ on The Shirelles' version.

The BBC version of 'Baby It's You' was a surprise no. 4 hit in the UK in 1994.

'Do You Want To Know A Secret?' (Lennon/McCartney)

Recorded 11 February 1963. George Harrison – lead vocals, acoustic guitar; John Lennon – acoustic guitar, backing vocals; Paul McCartney – bass, backing vocals; Ringo Starr – drums, percussion.

'Do You Want To Know A Secret?' was written by John Lennon, principally, in the weeks after his wedding in August 1962. He gave it to George, who sings in sincerely whilst employing his best Scouse burr.

'The tune was from a Disney movie,' Lennon told David Sheff in 1980. "Want to know a secret? Promise not to tell. You are standing by a wishing well.' ['I'm Wishing'] So, I had this sort of thing in my head and I wrote it and just gave it to George to sing. I thought it would be a good vehicle for him because it only had three notes and he wasn't the best singer in the world.'

George Harrison nominates The Stereos' 1961 hit, 'I Really Love You' as inspiration for the song. You can certainly sing the words of 'Do You Want To Know A Secret?' over the verse of 'I Really Love You', and there are some similar do-doos under the lead vocal of each.

As with 'Misery', 'Do You Want To Know A Secret?' starts with a slow introduction, which puts the listener off guard. Lennon only bothered writing one verse of lyrics which is used three times. 'Listen, do you want to know a secret? Do you promise not to tell? Closer. Let me whisper in your ear. Say the words you long to hear. I'm in love with you.' Thankfully, an inventive bridge and those parping 'do-wah-do' backing vocals in the second verse add some interest.

British listeners in mid-1963 might have been more familiar with the cover version by Billy J Kramer And The Dakotas, which was released as a single four weeks after *Please Please Me* and was held off number one by The Beatles' next single, 'From Me To You'.

'A Taste Of Honey' (Scott/Marlow)

Recorded 11 February 1963. Paul McCartney – lead vocals, bass; John Lennon – acoustic guitar, backing vocals; George Harrison – lead guitar, backing vocals; Ringo Starr – drums.

Whether through deliberate guile or McCartney's sweet tooth, 'A Taste Of Honey' effortlessly demonstrates the band's versatility. With 'I Saw Her Standing There' and 'Twist And Shout' book-ending the album with out-and-out rockers, they needed a slow number. Out came this Lenny Welch tune, which, as an instrumental version by Acker Bilk, sat just outside the UK top 20 on 11 February 1963.

'A Taste Of Honey' was the first song recorded in the afternoon session. It's the only waltz-time tune on the album, but needed five takes to perfect, with two further takes to complete double-tracked vocals. Ringo brushes his snares, George constructs a deft guitar accompaniment and Paul sings in his upper range brilliantly.

It's a beautiful and sweet song, proud of its Tin Pan Alley origins. John, for his part, seems to be suppressing a giggle the whole way through.

'There's A Place' (Lennon/McCartney)

Recorded 11 February 1963. John Lennon – vocals, harmonica, rhythm guitar; Paul McCartney – vocals, bass; George Harrison – backing vocals, lead guitar; Ringo Starr – drums

'There's A Place' is a candidate with 'What You're Doing' for the best lesser-known Beatles song. It was the first song recorded in their all-day session on 11 February 1963, and a series of outtakes reveal that they took a while to warm up, with the astounding vocal performances and Ringo's final drum arrangement only coming together as the morning progressed. Harmonica was added after lunch, its drop down the scale matching the intriguing and inward-looking lyrics.

There is a place
Where I can go
When I feel low
When I feel blue
And it's my mind

Parts might have been borrowed from *West Side Story*: 'There's a place for us, a time and place for us/Hold my hand and I'll take you there' ('Somewhere' by Leonard Bernstein and Stephen Sondheim).

The final take is anxious, tense and full of energy, with a thrilling split harmony on 'and it's my mind', which suggests teenage anxieties bursting forth. The song is just 1.52 in length. Boom!

'Twist And Shout' (Medley/Russell)

Recorded 11 February 1963. John Lennon – lead vocals, rhythm guitar; Paul McCartney – bass, backing vocals; George Harrison – lead guitar, backing vocals; Ringo Starr – drums.

'Twist And Shout' is pure rock and roll. Of all the songs on *Please Please Me*, it's this that most closely matches the power of their live concerts in Hamburg and Liverpool. But here, in the sterile studio environment, it's much more polite than any of their contemporary in-concert versions.

As the last song recorded during their all-day session for *Please Please Me*, you hear can John Lennon's larynx splitting apart in this bravado all-or-nothing, one-take blast through The Isley Brothers' 'Twist And Shout'. The original has a swing and a Latin touch – The Beatles convert this to out-and-out rock and roll. Here is the power and precision of The Beatles' live act, caught in three minutes at 10 pm on a Monday evening in a leafy north London street.

The famous vocal crescendo is John, George and Paul harmonising an A7 chord, as Dominic Pedler points out, 'John's A note (at 1.24), George's C# (at 1.27) and Paul's E (at 1.29) stack up, respectively, the root, major 3rd and 5th degrees of an A triad, before John extends the chord with a flat seventh by jumping to the high G (at 1.31). The result is an orgy of delicious dissonance almost guaranteed to send an audience into a frenzy.'

'Twist And Shout' was also used for judicious promotional opportunities. It was the final song of their *Sunday Night At The London Palladium* performance on 13 October 1963, the start of Beatlemania. It was also the song that followed John's cheeky 'rattle yer jewellery' crack at the Royal Command Performance on 4 November 1963, and was included in their crucial appearance on *The Ed Sullivan Show* on 9 February 1964.

Despite Giles Martin's terrific 2023 remix, we still prefer the adrenaline rush of the original mono. Whoo!

'From Me To You' b/w **'Thank You Girl'** (Single)

UK: 11 April 1963. US: 27 May 1963

Chart positions. UK: 1. US: did not chart.

'From Me to You' replaced Gerry And The Pacemakers' version of 'How Do You Do It?' at the top of the UK singles chart on 2 May 1963. This was The Beatles' first week of sixty-nine at the head of the UK 'hit parade' over the next six years. 'From Me To You' was number one for seven weeks, their joint-longest tenure with, perhaps surprisingly, 'Hello Goodbye'.

'From Me To You' (Lennon/McCartney)

Recorded 5 March 1963. John Lennon – vocals, rhythm guitar, harmonica; Paul McCartney – vocals, bass; George Harrison – lead guitar; Ringo Starr – drums.

Lennon and McCartney wrote 'From Me To You' on 28 February 1963 on a tour bus heading from York to Shrewsbury.

McCartney said in *The Lyrics: 1956 To The Present:*

> We were on tour with Roy Orbison [sic, it was Helen Shapiro] at the time we wrote this. 'We were all on the same tour bus, and it would stop somewhere so that people could go for a cup of tea and a meal, and John and I would have a cup of tea and then go back to the bus and write something. It was a special image to me, at twenty-one, to be walking down the aisle of the bus and there on the back seat of the bus is Roy Orbison, in black with his dark glasses, working on his guitar, writing 'Pretty Woman'. There was a camaraderie, and we were inspiring each other, which is always a lovely thing. He played the music for us, and we said, 'That's a good one, Roy. Great.' And then we'd say, 'Well, listen to this one,' and we'd play him 'From Me To You'. That was kind of a historic moment, as it turned out.

'From Me To You' is an attractive mix of pop and skiffle with a touch of blues. It displays all of the hallmarks of the early Beatles' sound: vocal harmonies, bursts of falsetto, the dramatic drum fills (as a transition back to the verses, we have Ringo's characteristic snare fill at 0.49, bettered by his thrilling 'backwards' trip around the tom-toms at 1.30), parping fills and personal pronouns. And yet, from those familiar components, we still get a fresh and timeless song.

And we also have the first inkling of an emerging willingness to push the boundaries of songwriting. At both 0.36 and 1.17, the song switches to a minor key on the word 'arms'. McCartney said in *Anthology*, 'I remember being very pleased with the middle eight because there was a strange chord in it, and it went into minor: 'I've got arms that long…' We thought that was a very big step. Our songwriting lifted a little with that song.' Some years later, in *Many Years From Now*, he would add: 'The thing I liked about 'From Me To You' was it had a very complete middle. It went to a surprising place. The opening chord of the middle section of that song heralded a new batch for me. That was a pivotal song.'

Indeed, as Dominic Pedler asserts, 'The result was an instant coming of age for The Beatles as songwriters' even as he admits that Buddy Holly's 'Raining In My Heart' uses the same change in the middle eight at 0.48 ('oh, *misery*, misery') and that The Beatles repeated the trick in 'I Want To Hold Your Hand' (and when I *touch you* I feel happy').

Written less than a week before it was recorded, 'From Me To You' was the first of eleven consecutive number-one singles in the UK over the next three-and-a-half years. They knew what they were doing.

As that Gm7 chord suggests, they were never happy with repeating themselves. From now on, The Beatles didn't just move forward with every new record, they moved fast, and everyone else followed.

'Thank You Girl' (Lennon/McCartney)

Recorded 5 March 1963. John Lennon – double-tracked vocals, rhythm guitar, harmonica; Paul McCartney – backing vocals, bass; George Harrison – lead guitar; Ringo Starr – drums.

Recorded on the same day as 'From Me To You', 'Thank You Girl' was intended as the follow-up single to 'Please Please Me'. It's a pleasing chugger of a song, but quite rightly not side one material.

Outtakes reveal Ringo's many attempts to get his drum fills in the outro just right. In the end, they added the final 22-second section as an edit piece, taking seven attempts (this is easily identified from 1.41 with slightly more reverb and a subtly increased tempo).

It's the first of a long series of songs that were released only as excellent B-sides and not on the band's main albums: 'I'll Get You', 'This Boy', 'She's A Woman', 'Yes It Is', 'I'm Down', 'Rain', 'The Inner Light', 'Revolution', 'Don't Let Me Down', 'Old Brown Shoe' and 'You Know My Name (Look Up The Number)'.

'She Loves You' b/w **'I'll Get You'** (single)

UK Single: 23 August 1963. US single: 16 September 1963.
Chart positions. UK: 1. US: 1.

The Beatles' fourth single, 'She Loves You', encapsulates 1963 in two minutes and twenty seconds. Simon Philo describes it as a 'thrilling jumble of percussion, guitars, voices, hooks, and harmonies that exploded into life in arresting fashion with the chorus, and simply did not stop exploding thereafter. Rich, sugary, and addictive, 'She Loves You' was dessert-only songwriting.'

Even today, more than sixty years later, 'She Loves You' is still the tenth best-selling single ever in the UK. With close to two million sales, all physical until 2009, it was the highest-selling UK single of all time until 1978, when it was replaced by 'Mull Of Kintyre'. With half a million pre-orders, 'She Loves You' remained in the charts for 31 consecutive weeks (that's seven months), with an 18-week residency in the top three between September and December 1963. It was number one twice: from 10 September for four weeks, and again for another four weeks after The Beatles featured on the bill of the prestigious Royal Variety Show, which drew twenty-six million viewers, approximately half the population, when televised on 10 November.

Seven months after its UK release, 'She Loves You' reached the top of the US charts, remaining there for two weeks in March 1964. 'She Loves You' was one of the five Beatles songs that held the top five positions in the US charts simultaneously on 4 April 1964.

Why? Take another listen.

'She Loves You' (Lennon/McCartney)

Recorded 1 July 1963. John Lennon – vocals, rhythm guitar; Paul McCartney – vocals, bass; George Harrison – backing vocals, lead guitar; Ringo Starr – drums.

'She Loves You', a 50-50 collaboration between John Lennon and Paul McCartney, was mostly written on 26 June 1963 in a room in the Turk's Hotel in Newcastle, prior to a performance at the Majestic Ballroom.

McCartney in *Anthology*: 'John and I wrote 'She Loves You' together. There was a Bobby Rydell song ['Forget Him'] out at the time and, as often happens, you think of one song when you write another. We were in a van up in Newcastle. I'd planned an 'answering song' where a couple of us would sing 'She loves you…' and the other one answers, 'Yeah, yeah.' We decided that that was a crummy idea as it was, but at least we then had the idea for a song called 'She Loves You'. So we sat in the hotel bedroom for a few hours and wrote it.'

Always pushing forward, whereas their previous three singles were written in the first person (in 'Love Me Do', 'Please Please Me' and 'From Me To You'), 'She Loves You' twists this into a third person narrative – as Paul told Barry Miles, 'It was again a she, you, me, I, personal preposition song. I suppose the most interesting thing about it was that it was a message song; it was someone bringing a message. It was moving off the 'I love you, girl' or 'Love me do'; it was a third person, which was a shift away. 'I saw her, and she said to me to tell you, that she loves you, so there's a little distance we managed to put in it, which was quite interesting.'

Five days later, 'She Loves You' and its B-side were recorded at EMI's Abbey Road studios.

It starts at a clip, bouncing immediately into the refrain with a burst of energy from the thumping floor tom. 'She Loves You' has an infectious and insistent 'yeah, yeah, yeah' hook, a powerful rhythm section (Ringo, perfect, as always) and a swooping harmony on 'can't be *bad*' borrowed from The Everly Brothers ('I'll cry each *time'* in Cathy's Clown'). The delirious falsetto 'whoo!' is capped by a magical G major sixth at the end. There is no bridge section and no harmonica – The Beatles were never too keen on repeating themselves – and 'She Loves You' establishes a pattern of new songs with nuances or sounds that no-one else could match. Over sixty years on it's difficult to imagine the incredible impact of 'She Loves You'. And this wasn't a one off – they would continue innovating for the next six years.

Writes Dominic Pedler:

> When it comes to pop perfection, 'She Loves You' represents a high-water mark in The Beatles story. A peak that, in terms of purity of concept and delivery, they would never top. 'Yesterday' may have clocked up more air-plays, 'In My Life' and 'Strawberry Fields' may have enjoyed more street credibility, 'Here, There And Everywhere' may be more musically intricate, and 'Lucy In The Sky With Diamonds' and 'Because' might indeed be more semantically challenging, but 'She Loves You' is surely the quintessential single on The Planet Earth jukebox. The evergreen themes of innocent young love, trepidation and expectancy found in the purest pop of any generation have never been captured so concisely.

Released in late August 1963, 'She Loves You' knocked another Lennon/McCartney song off the top of the charts on 10 September ('Bad To Me' by Billy J. Kramer And The Dakotas) and stayed in the top 10 for *the rest of the year.* Their appearance on *Val Parnell's Sunday Night At The London Palladium*, the UK's top TV variety show, on 13 October was televised live and watched by 15 million viewers. The Beatles topped the bill that night, closing the hour-long show. This pushed The Beatles into the mainstream. They performed 'From Me To You', 'I'll Get You', 'She Loves You' and 'Twist And Shout' and the newspaper coverage of screaming fans in the following days used the term 'Beatlemania' for the first time. They would record 'I Want To Hold Your Hand' four days later.

'She Loves You' was only planned as a mono single. George Martin didn't make a stereo mix of 'She Loves You' in 1963. Incredibly, the original two-track session tapes were erased, meaning that a true stereo mix from those tapes has never been possible. 'Love Me Do', 'P.S. I Love You' and 'I'll Get You' were similarly mistreated.

After a series of horrendous fake stereo mixes in 1964 (*The Beatles' Second Album*), 1966 (*A Collection Of Beatles' Oldies*) and 1973 (*1962-*

1966), advances in technology allowed Giles Martin to separate the elements of the mono mix and present a new stereo mix, released in 2023 as part of the expanded edition of *1962-1966*. We prefer the original mono, of course.

The German version, 'Sie Liebt Dich', is a wholly re-recorded new take. This was laid down in Paris on 29 January 1964 during sessions for 'Can't Buy Me Love'. The lyrics were translated by Camillo Felgen, a Luxembourgish singer, lyricist and television and radio presenter. Felgen, who used the nom-de-plume, Jean Nicolas, travelled to Paris to teach the phonetic pronunciations to The Beatles. Jo, jo, jo!

'I'll Get You' (Lennon/McCartney)

Recorded 1 July 1963. John Lennon – lead vocals, acoustic guitar, harmonica; Paul McCartney – lead vocals, bass; George Harrison – electric guitar, backing vocals; Ringo Starr – drums.

As with 'Thank You Girl', 'I'll Get You' was a candidate for the band's next A-side. It's perhaps too by the numbers to be a classic in its own right, with even more examples of 'yeah'. It's a duet, but John and Paul alternate between singing in unison (an octave apart) with occasional two-part harmony.

There is one interesting moment. As Lennon and McCartney sing 'It's not easy to pre*tend*...' the backing switches to a minor key. Although this was a trick that Paul borrowed from the opening line of 'All My Trials', a track from Joan Baez's debut album released in 1960, it was certainly a calculated and deliberately composed element offering a spark of novelty and craft in an otherwise work-a-day track.

There's also a mistake when John and Paul trip over the vocals in the middle eight. Lennon sings, 'I'm gonna make you mine', instead of 'gonna change your mind'. There is a second or two of confusion at 1.16 when one of them stops singing. This suggests that the song was dashed off in just a few takes, perhaps with only one full run-through.

As Alan Pollack suggests, 'I'll Get You' 'isn't necessarily not a 'good' song; merely that mapped against the steep growth trajectory they had so quickly established for themselves by this point, 'I'll Get You', if not entirely off the pace, surely catches them in the act of treading water.'

But even a rushed two-minute B-side shows all the hallmarks of their rapidly developing style and confidence. Oh yeah.

Twist And Shout EP

UK: 12 July 1963.

Chart position. UK: 1.

'Twist And Shout', 'A Taste Of Honey', 'Do You Want To Know A Secret', 'There's A Place'

The EP was a curious invention offering four tracks on a 7" disc. They were popular with buyers as you got four songs at a low price. The Beatles released 13 in total, two with exclusive tracks unavailable elsewhere. The first of these, *Twist And Shout,* outsold most singles for several weeks in 1963.

Contemporaneously, Brian Poole And The Tremeloes had a huge hit with 'Twist And Shout' themselves. As Poole told Spencer Leigh in *Love Me Do To Love Me Don't: Beatles On Record* (2016), 'we were doing 'Twist And Shout' on stage before we knew anybody else doing it and we felt we could have a hit with it. Unfortunately, we had it in the can for about a year before Decca decided to release it as a single'.

Nevertheless, 'Twist And Shout' was a million-seller for Brian Poole And The Tremeloes, reaching number 4 in a long chart run between July and October 1963.

With The Beatles (UK album)

22 November 1963.
Chart position. UK: 1.

If *Please Please Me* was recorded, for the most part, in a single day, sessions for its follow-up, *With The Beatles*, were squeezed in between their multitude of other commitments across three months in summer and autumn 1963.

Almost three weeks after recording 'She Loves You', the band returned to EMI for to start work on their second album. In the interim, they'd played seventeen concerts and recorded seven radio broadcasts.

Please Please Me was unavoidably recorded in a hurry. *With The Beatles* was recorded over seven sessions across three months. Many of the vocals would be double-tracked and piano was used on four tracks, and Hammond organ on a fifth. This adds new textures to an immaculately produced album that, for the most part, was recorded on a two-track console.

Holding back their original material for now, on 18 July they recorded covers of Smokey Robinson's 'You Really Got A Hold On Me', Barrett Strong's 'Money (That's What I Want)', The Donays' 'Devil In His Heart' and Meredith Willson's 'Till There Was You'. At the end of the month, on 30 July, they recorded the Marvelettes' 'Please Mr. Postman', their own 'It Won't Be Long', a remake of 'Till There Was You', a cover of Chuck Berry's 'Roll Over Beethoven' and Paul's wonderful 'All My Loving'. Incredibly they took a break mid-afternoon to travel three miles to the Playhouse Theatre to record six songs for BBC radio, before heading back to EMI for further sessions.

They returned to EMI on 11 September 1963 for 'Little Child', 'I Wanna Be Your Man', 'All I've Got To Do', 'Not A Second Time' and 'Don't Bother Me'. The next day they recorded 'Hold Me Tight', further takes of 'Little Child' and some overdubs to previous tracks. Further overdubs were completed on 30 September, 3 October and 23 October.

In the US, Capitol selected nine of these tracks – notably including all eight original songs – for *Meet The Beatles!*, adding 'I Want To Hold Your Hand', 'This Boy' and 'I Saw Her Standing There'.

'It Won't Be Long' (Lennon/McCartney)

Recorded 30 July 1963. John Lennon – double-tracked vocals, rhythm guitar; Paul McCartney – backing vocals, bass; George Harrison – backing vocals, lead guitar; Ringo Starr – drums.

The Beatles' second album doesn't start with the joyousness of '1-2-3-faw!' or the 'ching!' of 'A Hard Day's Night', but is no less memorable with an attention-grabbing, unaccompanied Lennon vocal, off-beat and double-tracked and reminiscent of Beethoven's Fifth symphony (da-da-da-daa).

The knowing call-and-response 'yeah! yeah! yeah!' backing vocals are straight from 'She Loves You' recorded earlier the same month. It's a *band* performance, with Ringo on top form, a grinding guitar riff which spookily anticipates 'Day Tripper' and Paul and George singing counterpoint under Lennon's blasting lead.

There's also an interesting chord change in the verse, from E to C ('Every night when *everybody* has fun'). This might have originated in Carl Perkins' 'Honey Don't' which has the same change in the verse after 'how come you say you will when you won't' or, as a move from A to F, in the bridge of Buddy Holly's 'Peggy Sue' ('Peggy Sue, Peggy Sue, *pretty*, pretty, pretty, pretty, Peggy Sue').

'Buddy Holly was sensational,' George Harrison told Alan Freeman on the US-syndicated radio show *Rock Around The World* in 1974. 'A little of that rubbed off in as much as I no longer have a fear of changing from A to F.'

The song ends, breathlessly and melodramatically, with four descending chords (G7 – F#7 – F7 – E) and wide-open barbershop harmonies, just like 'She Loves You'. 'It Won't Be Long' was never performed again outside the recording session but serves its purpose as a powerful and punchy album track, full of interest and invention.

John Lennon sings seven of the fourteen songs on *With The Beatles* (Paul and George have three each, Ringo one). In his four original songs, 'It Won't Be Long', 'All I've Gotta Do', 'Little Child' and 'Not A Second Time', the cheerfulness and upbeat nature of the melodies and arrangements hide an unconscious but deep sense of, loneliness or unhappiness: a longing for something more.

'All I've Got To Do' (Lennon/McCartney)

Recorded 11 September 1963. John Lennon – lead vocals, rhythm guitar; Paul McCartney – backing vocals, bass; George Harrison – backing vocals, lead guitar; Ringo Starr – drums.

For the dark and moody 'All I've Got To Do', John Lennon mixes Smokey Robinson and Arthur Alexander with hints of 'Baby It's You'. The opening chord (which does not reappear) comes straight from The Miracles' 6/8 doo-wop song from 1959 '(You Can) Depend On Me'. It's very distinctive, opening the song with a grand flourish.

The beautiful and wistful minor key chord progression in the verses (C#m – E – C#m – F#m – Am – E) switches to a more positive major key for the chorus. The lyrics reflect the music: romantic and longing in the verse, more forthright in the chorus.

Lennon's singing is peerless, in turns sensual and commanding, despite the deep-rooted sadness of the lyric and tone.

'All My Loving' (Lennon/McCartney)
Recorded 30 July 1963. Paul McCartney – double-tracked lead vocals, bass; John Lennon – backing vocals, rhythm guitar; George Harrison – backing and backing vocals, lead guitar; Ringo Starr – drums.
We're three songs in before Macca gets a lead vocal. And here is one of the greatest songs of the era, 'All My Loving'. The harmonies, chord progression and vocal performance are remarkable for a musician who has just turned 21.

As with 'It Won't Be Long' the introduction has an unaccompanied double-tracked lead vocal: 'close your eyes…' before the band tumble in with a walking blues bass line, an insistent triple-time rhythm guitar (probably borrowed from The Crystals' 'Da Doo Ron Ron' which was number 5 in the charts when 'All My Loving' was recorded) and a wonderful, self-confident singing performance by Paul. He harmonises with himself in the third verse.

The song was written for Jane Asher, but Paul seems to be singing directly to the band's fans: 'All my loving, I will send to you…' It was very popular. It was released as a single in the US in January 1964, as the lead track on an EP in the UK in February 1964 (number one for eight weeks in the UK and three weeks in Australia), and a chart-topper in its own right in Canada for five weeks, March-April 1964, replacing 'I Want To Hold Your Hand'. This Canadian version reached no. 45 in the US as import.

Completists can collect a German stereo mix which has a five beat hi-hat introduction.

'Don't Bother Me' (Harrison)
Recorded 12 September 1963. George Harrison – double-tracked vocals, lead guitar; John Lennon – rhythm guitar, tambourine; Paul McCartney – bass, claves; Ringo Starr – drums, bongos.
George Harrison's first serious composition is characteristically gloomy: John wasn't the only Beatle who felt melancholia. 'Don't Bother Me' was written in Bournemouth in August 1963 during the band's residency at the Gaumont cinema.

George was ill in bed and, with little else to do, began writing a song. He recorded himself on a portable tape recorder and a five-and-a-half minute long composing draft reveals his summer cold as he hums and whistles over the chord changes.

Just over three weeks later, The Beatles attempted to record 'Don't Bother Me' but failed to capture a useable take. They completed a new version the following evening. George's vocal was double-tracked during an overdub session.

Listen to the basic track, take 13, which reveals a few sweet, out-of-tune moments in George's lead vocal. The rest of the band added percussion. Lennon played a tambourine, McCartney claves, and Starr, an Arabian bongo.

The song is placed mid-way through side one, where it fits perfectly. George Martin was so skilled at sequencing Beatles' albums that any other running order just feels wrong.

In his 1980 memoir, *I, Me, Mine*, George writes, 'I don't think it's a particularly good song... It mightn't even be a song at all, but at least it showed me that all I needed to do was keep on writing, and then maybe eventually I would write something good.'

He was right. More, and better, Harrisongs would follow. 'Don't Bother Me' is not particularly memorable or inventive, but it's the beginning of something; satisfyingly 100% George. He didn't need to imitate John and Paul, and never would. From here we can trace a direct line through 'I Need You', 'Taxman', 'Something' and his magnum opus, *All Things Must Pass*.

'Little Child' (Lennon/McCartney)

Recorded 12 September 1963, 3 October 1963. John Lennon – vocals, rhythm guitar, harmonica; Paul McCartney – vocals, piano, bass; George Harrison – electric guitar; Ringo Starr – drums.

Written for Ringo, but sounding like The Rolling Stones, this is a pumping r&b song. Although The Beatles never played this live, you can get some idea of the excitement of a Cavern gig in 1962-1963: it's loud, rough and fun.

Paul cooks up a storm on piano, his first recorded performance on the instrument and John's twelve-bar blues harmonica solo is terrific, recorded as an edit piece and spliced into the take (0.54-1.11).

We'll skirt around the condescending lyrics, shall we?

'Till There Was You' (Willson)

Recorded 30 July 1963. Paul McCartney – vocals, bass; John Lennon – nylon-string guitar; George Harrison – nylon-string guitar; Ringo Starr – bongos.

Paul covers Peggy Lee with a song from the 1957 musical *The Music Man*. In their arrangement The Beatles upped the tempo a touch and simplified the arrangement for two electric guitars, bass and drums.

For their *With The Beatles* session, they switched to nylon-strung acoustic guitars and bongos, adding a delicate but bouncy Latin feel. Their beautiful arrangement, very different to the original, turns this into a *Beatles* song: harmony and melody reassigned from Broadway to Abbey Road. George's fluid, jazzy bossa nova guitar solo is one of his best, although it seems very carefully composed and one wonders whether Paul lent a hand. That solo includes a very particular chord, described by Dominic Pedler as 'a strikingly lush, dissonant G7#9 that hangs in splendid isolation (at 1.21). Meanwhile, on the *Live At The BBC* version the chord gets the full treatment, fluttering in and out of tune (at 1.22) courtesy of George's tasteful use of the vibrato bar.

Whether on the studio recordings or the live *Anthology* footage, the novelty of this chord is unmistakable.'

Paul spoke about this enthusiastically in *Many Years From Now*: 'That was a chord we used twice in The Beatles. It was a chord shown to us by Jim Gretty, who worked behind the counter at Frank Hessey's, where we used to buy our instruments on the 'never never' in Liverpool. So Jim Gretty showed us this one great ham-fisted jazz chord, bloody hell! George and I learned it off him…'

For the record, the other time it was used was in 'Michelle', just before 'ma belle' in the opening seconds.

By mid-1963 'Till There Was You' had been in the band's set for a couple of years and was rolled out when they needed to display their versatility: as part of their unsuccessful audition for Decca in January 1962, for example (Pete Best's tempo speeds up noticeably as the songs progresses and Paul sounds very nervous), during their first appearance on *The Ed Sullivan Show* in February 1964 and in their first American live show that same month.

'Please Mr. Postman' (Dobbins/Garrett/Gorman/Holland/Bateman)
Recorded 30 July 1963. John Lennon – double-tracked vocals, rhythm guitar; Paul McCartney – backing vocals, bass; George Harrison – backing vocals, lead guitar; Ringo Starr – drums.

Such was the competition in Liverpool's lively dance hall and club scene in 1961-1962, with hundreds of bands all playing the same songs, The Beatles would constantly try and find something new and different. This was one of their strengths: choosing cover versions that nobody else knew. 'Please Mr. Postman' is a fine example of a killer song that was included in their first-ever session for the BBC, recorded in Manchester on 7 March 1962. As historian Mark Lewisohn writes, 'The Beatles' spot on [BBC radio's] *Here We Go* didn't appear to herald anything exceptional. It wasn't anticipated in the music press, they received a name-only billing in the BBC's programme journal *Radio Times*, and the broadcast won no retrospective notice as a special moment. But it was. After identifying John Lennon as the singer of 'Memphis, Tennessee', presenter Ray Peters labelled it 'a rhythm and blues version'. Such words would have been unfamiliar to the studio and listening audience – in fact, so seldom was r&b heard on the BBC that, for many, this would have been their initial exposure to something new. And when John sang 'Please Mr Postman' [originally by The Marvelettes] it was both the first time this song had been broadcast and the first time anything from Tamla had been played on BBC radio. Without even realising it (and they'd have been thrilled to know), The Beatles broke the Detroit 'Motown sound' to the British listening public.'

The Beatles' version is magnificent: sung brilliantly. Their performance is especially impressive as it was one of five songs recorded on 30 July 1963 (the others were 'It Won't Be Long', 'Till There Was You', 'Roll Over Beethoven', and 'All My Loving').

It would be another two years before Mary Wells' 'My Guy' would become Motown's first hit single in the UK. Once again, The Beatles got there first.

'Roll Over Beethoven' (Berry)

Recorded 30 July 1963. George Harrison – double-tracked vocals, lead guitar, handclaps; John Lennon – rhythm guitar, handclaps; Paul McCartney – bass, handclaps; Ringo Starr – drums, handclaps.

Peter Jackson's *Get Back* documentary revealed many surprises. One of them was confirmation of their vast knowledge of songs, retained from their Hamburg residencies between 1960 and 1962. When we watch the band just noodling around, it's clear that they knew dozens of songs, honed over hundreds of performance hours. 'Roll Over Beethoven' was one of fifteen songs written by Chuck Berry that were part of their live set. They performed more Berry covers than any other songwriter, although they only recorded two of these for EMI (the other was 'Rock And Roll Music'). The Beatles, of course, refashioned these songs in their own image.

'Roll Over Beethoven' is a basic twelve-bar rock-and-roll song, simple enough be to a staple of their set from the earliest Quarry Men concerts when it was sung by John Lennon. It became a George Harrison vocal vehicle in 1961. By 1963, they had been playing it for five years and needed just five takes to lay down a bright, tight version with an overdubbed second lead vocal and a tagged-on final guitar chord. The 2023 stereo remix pushes the drums forward. Ringo's precision and power are not generally recognised but, wow, he was good.

The studio version does sound a little safe and sterile, though. It was on the stage that this song flourished. Compare the live performances for Swedish TV in October 1963 (available on *Anthology 1*) and at the Hollywood Bowl in August 1964 (when Paul adds a high harmony on the last verse). Wonderful.

'Hold Me Tight' (Lennon/McCartney)

Recorded 12 September 1963. Paul McCartney – vocals, bass, handclaps; John Lennon – backing vocals, rhythm guitar, handclaps; George Harrison – backing vocals, lead guitar, handclaps; Ringo Starr – drums, handclaps.

'Hold Me Tight' had been recorded in thirteen takes for *Please Please Me* in February but was redone for *With The Beatles*.

It is generally regarded as a weak song, which seems unfair. Outtakes from the 12 September session reveal that Paul was having trouble remembering the words – his bass playing is so lively that he is on the verge of losing control of his singing – and John, as so often, was uncertain in his cueing. You can hear him laughing at his mistakes. In the end, producer George Martin edited the best two takes together.

As with all of the original mixes of the early albums, the bass and drums are mixed low to avoid issues with tiny speakers on radios and record players. Boost the bass and play it loud.

'You Really Got A Hold On Me' (Robinson)

Recorded 18 July 1963. John Lennon – rhythm guitar, lead vocals; George Harrison – lead guitar, lead vocals; Paul McCartney – bass, backing vocals; Ringo Starr – drums; George Martin – piano.

The depth of The Beatles' knowledge of American soul and r&b is evident here. 'You Really Got A Hold On Me' was a B-side by The Miracles released at the end of 1962. One could argue that its subject matter links back to the self-pity observed in 'All I've Go To Do' and 'Little Child' (and the earlier 'Ask Me Why' and 'Misery').

Recorded for the BBC in May and July 1963, they were keen enough to make this the first song recorded for *With The Beatles*. It is a wonderful band performance with a sparkling stop-start arrangement, brilliant harmonies, a killer lead vocal from John Lennon (much more intense than Smokey Robinson's silky tenor) and George Martin on piano. The final version is a seamless edit of takes 7, 10 and 11.

As with 'Please Mr Postman', this is full of *soul*, and in 1963, this was one of The Beatles' USPs.

'I Wanna Be Your Man' (Lennon/McCartney)

Recorded 12 September 1963, 3 October 1963, 23 October 1963. Ringo Starr – double-tracked vocals, drums; John Lennon – backing vocals, rhythm guitar; Paul McCartney – backing vocals, bass; George Harrison – backing vocals, lead guitar; George Martin – Hammond organ.

Famously quickly written for The Rolling Stones, mostly on a single chord and borrowing in places from their version of Bobby Spellman's 'Fortune Teller', 'I Wanna Be Your Man' was Ringo's lead vocal for *With The Beatles*. It's a rudimentary rock 'n' roll song, easy to play and sing, but lifted by Paul's evident enthusiasm. Ringo nails the groove, loud and true. 'I Wanna Be Your Man' was simple and exciting enough to be performed on-stage for the next three years. Listen for George Martin vamping on the Hammond organ from 1:46 as the song threatens to turn into a lively blues jam.

The Rolling Stones recorded their version on 7 October and released it as their second single on 1 November, three weeks ahead of *With The Beatles*.

'Devil In Her Heart' (Drapkin)

Recorded 18 July 1963. George Harrison – double-tracked vocals, lead guitar; John Lennon – backing vocals, rhythm guitar; Paul McCartney – backing vocals, bass; Ringo Starr – drums, maracas.

This is George's second lead vocal on the album, covering a song by the female vocal group The Donays from Detroit, the B-side of their only single, 'Bad Boy' (not the song recorded by The Beatles in 1965).

It's the very definition of 'filler', but 'Devil In Her Heart' has a small place in the Beatles' legend as the last 'girl group' cover version recorded by the band. The move from female to male protagonist necessitated a change of title from

'(There's A) Devil In His Heart' and a big drop in key from E to G. This key change affects the whole feel of the song.

Both The Donays and their composer/producer Richard Drapkin might be all but forgotten, but 'Devil In Her Heart' is immortal as a song by the best band of all.

'Not A Second Time' (Lennon/McCartney)

Recorded 11 September 1963. John Lennon – double-tracked vocals, acoustic guitar; Paul McCartney – bass; George Harrison – acoustic guitar; Ringo Starr – drums; George Martin – piano.

Another suffering-in-love song from John Lennon ('You hurt me then, you're back again/no, not a second time'). Lennon generally wrote about himself, and although pop songs don't necessarily stand over-analysis, there's a high ratio of hurt songs in The Beatles' early albums.

Acoustic guitars and piano add texture to a composition with an irregular format: fourteen-bar verses and a ten-bar chorus. John Lennon wrote intuitively, with no regard to musical rules. The asymmetry of 'Not A Second Time' is overlaid with unusual chord changes. This was noticed by *The Times*' music critic William Mann in an article 'What Songs The Beatles Sang' published on 27 December 1963.

> Harmonic interest is typical of their quicker songs, too, and one gets the impression that they think simultaneously of harmony and melody, so firmly are the major tonic sevenths and ninths built into their tunes, and the flat submediant key switches, so natural is the Aeolian cadence at the end of 'Not A Second Time' (the chord progression which ends Mahler's 'Song of the Earth').

Music scholars have failed to agree just what Mann was trying to put across. Dominic Pedler suggests that 'any connection between ['Not A Second Time' and 'Song Of The Earth'] is at best tenuous and at worst, completely baffling.'

As Lennon told Jan Wenner in 1970:

> There is a guy in England, William Mann, who was the first intellectual who reviewed The Beatles in *The Times* and got people talking about us in that intellectual way. He wrote about Aeolian cadences and all sorts of musical terms, and he is a bullshitter. But he made us credible with intellectuals. He wrote about Paul's last album [*McCartney*] as if it were written by Beethoven or something. He's still writing the same shit. But it did us a lot of good in that way, because people in all the middle classes and intellectuals were all going 'Oooh'.

And, years later, he remarked: 'To this day, I don't have any idea what [Aeolian cadences] are. They sound like exotic birds.'

'Not A Second Time' would lead, indirectly, to the complexity of songs such as 'If I Fell', 'You've Got To Hide Your Love Away' and others. Its irregular structure proved that, as Pedler writes, 'from the very early days, The Fab Four were dictating that pop melodies need no longer be so regimentally restricted to four-bar and eight-bar phrases within a strict 4/4 metre. If the lyric and the melody suggested adding or dropping beats then The Beatles would make the bar structure adapt as necessary. 'Not A Second Time' demonstrates a melodic revolution in the making.'

'Money (That's What I Want)' (Bradford/Gordy)

Recorded 18 July 1963. John Lennon – vocals, rhythm guitar; Paul McCartney – backing vocals, bass; George Harrison – backing vocals, lead guitar; Ringo Starr – drums; George Martin – piano.

The third Motown cover on *With The Beatles*, 'Money (That's What I Want)', attempts to outrave 'Twist And Shout' and damn near succeeds.

George Harrison: 'Brian [Epstein] had had a policy at NEMS of buying at least one copy of every record that was released. If it sold, he'd order another one, or five or whatever. Consequently he had records that weren't hits in Britain, weren't even hits in America. Before going to a gig, we'd meet in the record store, after it had shut, and we'd search the racks like ferrets to see what new ones were there … 'Devil In Her Heart' and Barrett Strong's 'Money' were records that we'd picked up and played in the shop and thought were interesting.'

The song is powered by a full-throated vocal from John Lennon, close call-and-response harmonies from George Harrison and Paul McCartney, some politely rocking piano by George Martin and a brilliant performance from Ringo Starr, who sticks to his tom-toms until the last choruses when his eight-to-the-bar bass drumming drives to an exciting conclusion.

'Oh yeah, I wanna be free,' Lennon shouts – not an extemporization, even if it sounds like it, but taken straight from Barrett Strong's 1959 original.

The Beatles' Hits EP (UK)

6 September 1963.
Chart position. UK: 1.
'From Me to You', 'Thank You Girl', 'Please Please Me, 'Love Me Do' (single version)

The Beatles (No.1) EP

UK: 1 November 1963.
Chart position. UK: 2.
'I Saw Her Standing There', 'Misery', 'Anna (Go To Him)', 'Chains'

'I Want To Hold Your Hand' b/w **'This Boy'** (UK single)
'I Want To Hold Your Hand' b/w **'I Saw Her Standing There'** (US single)

UK: 29 November 1963. US: 26 December 1963.
Chart position. UK: 1. US: 1.
The big one: 'I Want To Hold Your Hand' was the song that broke The Beatles worldwide. Before that, the song generated 1,000,000 advance orders in the UK – mind-boggling when around 100,000 sales would give you a number one hit in the pre-streaming era.

Unsurprisingly, 'I Want To Hold Your Hand' would be number one in the UK for six weeks in December 1963 and January 1964, and (with a different B-side) it would top the charts in the US for seven weeks in February and March.

Throughout 1963 there had been 110 different acts who registered an entry in the *Billboard* Top 10. Over 100 of these were American, with one-off hits from Australia (Rolf Harris), Belgium (The Singing Nun), Brazil, Cuba, Denmark and Japan. The sole UK-based hit across the whole of 1963 was 'You Don't Have To Be A Baby To Cry' by the duo The Caravelles. This compares with the last three-quarters of 1964 when 26 different UK acts hit the top ten in America. 'I Want To Hold Your Hand' was the catalyst, seven weeks at number one in the US, as well as number one in Australia, Denmark, The Netherlands, New Zealand, Norway, Sweden and West Germany.

'I Want To Hold Your Hand' (Lennon/McCartney)
Recorded 17 October 1963. John Lennon – vocals, rhythm guitar, handclaps; Paul McCartney – vocals, bass, handclaps; George Harrison – lead guitar, handclaps; Ringo Starr – drums, handclaps.
What might sound like a simple song is deceptively complex. Here was The Beatles' strength as songwriters: the abrupt introduction, the push to the verse, the trademark two-part harmony in 'oh yeah I…', George's little guitar fills, the handclaps, the throbbing climb to 'hold your *hand*', the drop in dynamics in the eleven-bar bridge ('and when I touch you'), the 'I can't hide' vocals over the introduction chords, in which Paul forces himself into his highest register, and, breathlessly after two-and-half-minutes, the surprising deceleration of the triple-time ending, with no fade-out.

And yet, it is effortlessly commercial. And it makes you feel good.

For the first time, George Martin was able to record The Beatles in four-track. Writes Jerry Hammack:

> The move to four-track could be viewed in a couple of lights historically. Pop producers in the US routinely used three and four-track machines to exert more control over their sound, not discounting the fact that stereo releases were much more prominent in the US market. Simply to be competitive in the quality of recordings they produced, EMI would have had to eventually make the move beyond twin-track. In terms of engineering, it was also simply much easier to produce the increasingly layered recordings pop acts were producing using four-track. Decisions about how to arrange

the recording process and schedule musicians to facilitate different arrangements, as well as recording songs non-contiguously, was also made easier with the move to four-track.

Having invested in a Telefunken M10 (replaced by a Studer J37 the following year), EMI were unwilling to progress beyond four-track recording for the next five years: all of The Beatles' recordings at Abbey Road were squeezed onto four-track until mid-way through sessions for *The Beatles* in 1968.

The German language version, 'Komm, Gib Mir Deine Hand', credited to Lennon-McCartney-Nicolas-Hellmer, was released as a single in West Germany in the early weeks of 1964. This would see the US release on the *Something New* album on 20 July 1964, but would not be available in the UK until the *Rarities* album in November 1978.

'This Boy' (Lennon/McCartney)

Recorded 17 October 1963. John Lennon – double-tracked lead vocals, acoustic guitar; Paul McCartney – backing vocals, bass; George Harrison – backing vocals, electric guitar; Ringo Starr – drums.

In the US, it was the rocking 'I Saw Her Standing There' that would be placed as the B-side of 'I Want To Hold Your Hand'. In the UK, and therefore the band's artistic statement, it was 'This Boy', which uses the doo-wop guitar chord progression in waltz time and a glorious three-part harmony to combine into one of The Beatles' best-ever B-sides. Its progenitor was most likely 'I've Been Good To You' by John's favourite, The Miracles which is in the same time signature and uses a very similar chord pattern. George spoke also of the influence of the American vocal bands Frankie Lymon And The Teenagers and The Platters. He explained further in *Anthology*. 'When you think back to early rock and roll,' he said, 'there was always stuff like Frankie Lymon and The Teenagers, The Everly Brothers, The Platters. Everybody had harmonies; it was natural to sing a harmony sometimes.'

The calm 'this Boy/that boy' verses with those glorious vocals are split by an intense, agitated bridge in which John Lennon sings magnificently – it's one of the great rock voices in full flight. Listen to the middle section of 'You Don't Understand Me' by Bobby Freeman for the likely inspiration for this goosebumps moment.

And they tuck this away on a B-side?

1964

Introducing ... The Beatles (US album)

10 January 1964.
Chart position. US: 2.
'I Saw Her Standing There'; 'Misery'; 'Anna (Go To Him)'; 'Chains'; 'Boys'; 'Love Me Do'; 'P.S. I Love You'; 'Baby It's You'; 'Do You Want To Know A Secret'; 'A Taste Of Honey'; 'There's A Place'; 'Twist And Shout'
A second version replaces 'Love Me Do' with 'Ask My Why' and 'P.S. I Love You' with 'Please Please Me'.

It's hard to believe now, but Capitol Records, EMI's American subsidiary, rejected the *Please Please Me* album. Instead, George Martin placed the album with Vee-Jay, who can hardly have believed their luck when 'I Want To Hold Your Hand' broke The Beatles in America in early 1964. *Introducing... The Beatles* comprises most of the *Please Please Me* album. It seems that Vee Jay failed to realise that they didn't have the rights to either 'Love Me Do' or its B-side.

It was a hugely popular album, but lacking that huge hit single, it took a little longer to register in the charts, by which time Capitol's album had been released and reached number one.

Capitol licenced these songs to Vee Jay until the end of 1964, by which time it had sold more than 1.3 million copies. The album *The Early Beatles* followed soon afterwards, comprising ten songs from *Introducing... The Beatles*.

Meet The Beatles! (US album)

20 January 1964.
Chart position. US: 1.
'I Want to Hold Your Hand', 'I Saw Her Standing There', 'This Boy', 'It Won't Be Long', 'All I've Got to Do', 'All My Loving', 'Don't Bother Me', 'Little Child', 'Till There Was You', 'Hold Me Tight', 'I Wanna Be Your Man', 'Not a Second Time'
Capitol quicky realised their mistake and for the next three years, would plunder and pillage the UK releases for their own series of albums and singles. This went against The Beatles' artistic intentions and annoyed them considerably. It was only when their record contract was renewed in early 1967 that The Beatles were able to insist that their albums and singles released as they wanted. Even then, Capitol managed to put out two albums in the back half of their career, which had no direct UK equivalents.

So, for American audiences, this was The Beatles' first album. It set a precedent. US albums generally included only 12 tracks, two fewer than British releases. It was expected that the latest hit single would also be included . By shuffling and/or omitting tracks across a series of releases between late 1963 and mid-1966, the six British albums (which, of course, represent the band's vision of how they wanted their music to be presented) were re-worked into ten in the US.

Nevertheless, these were very popular. *Meet The Beatles!* sold over four million copies in 1964. To a generation of American listeners this is how they remember first listening to their favo(u)rite band.

'Please Please Me' b/w **'From Me To You'** (US single)
30 January 1964.
Chart position. US: 3.

All My Loving EP (UK)
7 February 1964.
Chart position. UK: 1.
'All My Loving', 'Ask Me Why', 'Money (That's What I Want)', 'P.S. I Love You'

'Twist And Shout' b/w **'There's A Place'** (US single)
2 March 1964.
Chart position. US: 2.

'Can't Buy Me Love' b/w **'You Can't Do That'** (single)
UK: 20 March 1964. US: 16 March 1964.
Chart positions. UK: 1. US: 1.
It might not be obvious to casual listeners, but both sides of The Beatles' first single of 1964 are based on the blues. Were they aware of The Rolling Stones peering over their shoulders? 'Not Fade Away', the London group's first big hit, was recorded on 10 January, two weeks before the first session for 'Can't Buy Me Love'. By the time the song was finished, and the B-side recorded also, 'Not Fade Away' was already in the shops.

'Can't Buy Me Love' (Lennon/McCartney)
Recorded 29 January and 25 February 1964. Paul McCartney – double-tracked vocals, bass; John Lennon – acoustic guitar; George Harrison – double-tracked lead guitar, 12-string guitar; Ringo Starr – drums.
Trivia question: which was the first Beatles song for EMI that was partially recorded outside the UK?

Answer: 'Can't Buy Me Love'.

Twenty-one months after their Hamburg sessions for Bert Kaempfert, and mid-way through a residency at L'Olympia in Paris, The Beatles were called to record German-language versions of their two previous singles. They were so efficient that there was time to record four takes of their newly-written sixth single. An edit of two of these takes can be heard on *Anthology 1*.

Returning to London after their huge successes on Ed Sullivan's *'Shew'*, work continued at EMI with vocal and guitar overdubs. With production of the film *A Hard Day's Night* due to begin on the afternoon of Monday, 2 March 1964, The Beatles spent four productive days recording the songs that would be performed in the film, along with two tracks for an EP and their next single.

> Tuesday, 25 February: 'You Can't Do That' (nine takes), 'And I Love Her' (version 1, two takes), 'I Should Have Known Better' (three takes), 'Can't Buy Me Love' (overdubs)
>
> Wednesday, 26 February: 'I Should Have Known Better' (nineteen takes), 'And I Love Her' (version 2, nine takes)
>
> Thursday, 27 February: 'And I Love Her' (version 3, two takes), 'If I Fell' (fifteen takes), 'Tell Me Why' (eight takes)
>
> Sunday, 1 March: 'I'm Happy Just To Dance With You' (four takes) plus 'Long Tall Sally' (one take) and 'I Call Your Name' (seven takes)

That's nine complete songs in four days against extreme time pressures.

Filming continued for the next seven weeks until 24 April. On a rare day off, they convened at EMI to record John Lennon's title song. Just who suggested 'A Hard Day's Night' as the title is open to different claimants, but Lennon was quick off the mark to write the song which would be the band's next single.

But first, 'Can't Buy Me Love'.

As with 'She Loves You', 'Can't Buy Me Love' opens, energetically and exuberantly, with the refrain. It's like jumping on a train at full speed. The song then follows a variant 12-bar blues structure. This is such a rarity in the band's original material, only fifteen of their songs, that it is notable. Likewise, there are none of the distinctive vocal harmonies that were such a key part of the first five singles. The blueprint for the verses seems to be Little Richard's 'Lucille', which they performed in concert between 1957 and 1962 and recorded twice for BBC radio in September 1963 – a few weeks before their Paris session. The chorus journeys around the Cycle of Fifths, a songwriter's staple technique familiar from standards like 'Moon River' and 'Fly Me To The Moon'. Dominic Pedler:

> The Beatles first transformed its use in pop in the chorus of 'Can't Buy Me Love', where it created a stunning contrast alongside the unadulterated 12-bar blues of the verse.

This was an important song for The Beatles. At their first session for 'Can't Buy Me Love', this was just their next single. Everything would change a few days later when 'I Want To Hold Your Hand' became their first US number one. By the second session, they had been number one for four weeks. 'Can't Buy Me Love' therefore needed to perform. When it reached number one on 4 April 1964, The Beatles held the entire top five on the Hot 100. No other act had held the top five spots simultaneously, and no-one would again in the pre-streaming era. In September 2021, Canadian rapper Drake held all five top spots, with 'Way 2 Sexy' at number one. Just over a year later, Taylor Swift occupied the entire top 10 [5 November 2022: number one, 'Anti-Hero']. But, as so often, The Beatles did it first. And, arguably, best.

Trivia question: which was the second and last Beatles song for EMI that was partially recorded outside the UK? Answer: 'The Inner Light'.

'You Can't Do That' (Lennon/McCartney)

Recorded 25 February 1964. John Lennon – lead vocals, electric guitar; Paul McCartney – backing vocals, bass, cowbell; George Harrison – backing vocals, electric 12-string guitar; Ringo Starr – drums, bongos.

A chiming 12-string guitar – the first time it was heard on a Beatles recording – opens this hard-edged, rhythmic John Lennon song. Here is an early indication of The Beatles, or George Harrison at least, striving for new sounds. This would be pushed further on their forthcoming album with overdubbed Paul's piano ('Any Time At All' and 'When I Get Home') and John and George playing nylon-string guitars ('And I Love Her' and 'I'll Be Back').

Lyrically, 'You Can't Do That' is one of a series in 1964 that focuses on jealousy and self-pity. These themes are reflected in other contemporary songs such as 'I'll Cry Instead' and 'Tell Me Why' (and, a little later, 'I'm A Loser' and 'I Don't Want To Spoil The Party'). And whereas McCartney, in early 1964, wrote about diamond rings and sex, Lennon went straight for the emotional jugular.

So please listen to me if you want to stay mine
I can't help my feelings, I go out of my mind

There's an uncomfortable whiff of paranoia, even misogyny, here. Different times.

You cannot doubt Lennon's sincerity in his throaty singing – as though he's going to miss those higher notes but gets there just to spite the listener.

As with 'Can't Buy Me Love', the verses in 'You Can't Do That' follow the twelve-bar blues form, extended to four repetitions and lots of seventh notes. In his famous 1980 *Playboy* interview, Lennon said: 'That's me doing a Wilson Pickett song. You know, a cowbell going four in the bar, and that chord going chatoong.'

'That chord' is probably the one that underpins 'but I told you before', just before the title, 'oh, you can't do that.' At that point the song's message is heard loud and clear.

Take a listen to Pickett's 'Peace Breaker' for a possible blueprint.

'Do You Want To Know A Secret?' b/w **'Thank You Girl'** (US single)

23 March 1964.

Chart position. US: 2.

Souvenir Of Their Visit To America EP (US)
23 March 1964
'Misery', 'A Taste of Honey', 'Ask Me Why', 'Anna (Go To Him)'

The Beatles' Second Album (US album)
10 April 1964.
Chart position. US: 1.
'Roll Over Beethoven', 'Thank You Girl', 'You Really Got a Hold on Me', 'Devil in Her Heart', 'Money (That's What I Want)', 'You Can't Do That', 'Long Tall Sally', 'I Call Your Name', 'Please Mr. Postman', 'I'll Get You', 'She Loves You'
Tracks from *With The Beatles*, the *Long Tall Sally* EP, three B-sides and an old single make up the second Capitol album which replaced *Meet The Beatles!* at the top of the Billboard album charts. By chance, it collects the best of the band's early soul and rock 'n' roll originals and covers: this is a very fine collection of songs.

Four By The Beatles EP (US)
11 May 1964.
Chart position. US: 92.
'Roll Over Beethoven', 'All My Loving', 'This Boy', 'Please Mr. Postman'

'Sie Liebt Dich' b/w **'I'll Get You'** (US single)
21 May 1964.
Chart position. US: 97.

Long Tall Sally EP (UK)
UK: 19 June 1964.
Chart position. UK: 1.
Such was the demand for new Beatles material in 1964, and such was their productivity, that they recorded four songs exclusively for an EP – a popular format when new albums cost well over £1, way beyond the budget of most teenagers.

In the US, 'Long Tall Sally' and 'I Call Your Name' had been released on *The Beatles' Second Album* (10 April 1964), with 'Matchbox' and 'Slow Down' added to *Something New* (20 July 1964). In Canada, the title track gave its name to an intriguing album called *The Beatles' Long Tall Sally* which comprised 'I Want To Hold Your Hand', 'I Saw Her Standing There', 'You Really Got A Hold On Me', 'Devil In Her Heart', 'Roll Over Beethoven', 'Misery', 'Long Tall Sally', 'I Call Your Name', 'Please Mr. Postman', 'This Boy', 'I'll Get You' And 'You Can't Do That'.

Outside the UK and US, the four songs were released wherever they would fit commercial demands. In Italy, for example, they appeared on a 1965 Parlophone compilation album called *The Beatles In Italy,* along with A-sides and B-sides from four singles.

'Long Tall Sally' (Johnson/Penniman/Blackwell)

Recorded 1 March 1964. Paul McCartney – bass, lead vocals; John Lennon – rhythm guitar; George Harrison – lead guitar; Ringo Starr – drums.

One take. That's all it took for Macca to lay down this genuine, stirring, exuberant blast of Little Richard. The energy is so high that they kept Paul's obvious flubs in verses two and three (on 'bald-headed Sally' and 'built for speed').

'Long Tall Sally' would be part of the band's set for nine years, from 1957, when Paul joined, through to their very last fee-paying concert at Candlestick Park, San Francisco, on 29 August 1966. Almost forty years later, on 14 August 2014, Paul McCartney returned to become the last musician to perform at Candlestick Park before its demolition the following year. He sang 'Long Tall Sally' as part of his encore, naturally, and *just about* hit the high notes.

'I Call Your Name' (Lennon/McCartney)

Recorded 1 March 1964. John Lennon – lead vocals, rhythm guitar; Paul McCartney – bass; George Harrison – 12-string lead guitar; Ringo Starr – drums, cowbell.

'I Call Your Name' was given to Billy J Kramer And The Dakotas, and recorded by them at EMI on 27 June 1963. It was released as the B-side to 'Bad To Me', another Lennon-McCartney original. Kramer does his best to add some soul to his version, but he was never a strong singer.

Lennon adds some grit to The Beatles' version, as well as replacing the brief rave-up in Kramer's recording with a remarkable ska/bluebeat instrumental section. It's no coincidence that Millie's 'My Boy Lollipop' was released around the time of the recording sessions for 'I Call Your Name' – it would be a big hit in April and May 1964 and still be in the top 20 when the *Long Tall Sally* EP was made available.

There are four distinct mix variants of 'I Call Your Name'. For collectors and Beatles nerds, they are:

Mono mix, 4 March 1964, released on *The Beatles' Second Album*. The cowbell starts at 0.01 with the drums. The guitar solo is edited at 1.08, after the line 'I call your name'. A cowbell is heard through this line of vocal.

Stereo mix, 10 March 1964, released on *The Beatles' Second Album*. The cowbell starts at 0.09 on the word 'call'. The guitar solo is edited at 1.06, before the line 'I call your name'. The cowbell is not heard through this line of vocal.

Mono mix, 4 June 1964, released on *Long Tall Sally* EP. The cowbell starts at 0.01 with the drums. The guitar solo is edited at 1.06, before the line 'I call your name'. The cowbell is not heard through this line of vocal.

Mono mix, 22 June 1964, released on *Rock & Roll Music And Past Masters*. The cowbell starts at 0.11 immediately before the line 'but you're not there'. The guitar solo is edited at 1.08, after the line 'I call your name'. The cowbell is heard through this line of vocal.

'Slow Down' (Williams)
Recorded 1 and 4 June 1964. John Lennon – lead vocals, lead guitar; Paul McCartney – bass; George Harrison –rhythm guitar; Ringo Starr – drums.
This cover of Larry William's 'Slow Down' has little of the spit and grind of the 1957 original. The honking saxophones are replaced by a perfunctory guitar solo and even Lennon's final 'whoo' sounds forced. Listen to the original stereo mix, with drums, bass, guitars and vocals panned hard left. Ringo's playing is perfection, right in the groove with energy and personality, with snare fills at 0.45 and 2.43 and fabulous characteristic tom-tom flourishes at 1.18 and 2.25. The right channel showcases George Martin's terribly polite piano playing and a poor edit at 1.14 when two takes are combined.

'Matchbox' (Perkins)
Recorded 1 June 1964. Ringo Starr – vocals, drums; John Lennon – rhythm guitar; Paul McCartney – bass; George Harrison – lead guitar.
If 'Slow Down' was a new low for The Beatles, then 'Matchbox', recorded earlier the same day, must be there or thereabouts.

'Matchbox' was in the band's set in 1961 and 1962, sung by Pete Best and, later, John Lennon. A tired live version from the band's final dates at the Star-Club in December 1962 can be heard on 1977's *Live! At The Star-Club In Hamburg, Germany, 1962* complete with Lennon vocal and ragged guitar solo.

This 1964 version has little to commend it. Ringo's voice is shot, even by his own standards (he would be hospitalised with acute tonsillitis a couple of days after the session), which even swathes of reverb and hit-and-miss double-tracking cannot disguise. George emulates his hero Carl Perkins with elan and style.

Astoundingly, Capitol saw fit to release 'Matchbox' as a single on 24 August 1964, with 'Slow Down' on the B-side. It reached number 25 on the *Billboard* Hot 100 singles chart.

A Hard Day's Night (US album)

26 June 1964.
Chart position. US: 1.
'A Hard Day's Night', 'Tell Me Why', 'I'll Cry Instead', 'I Should Have Known Better [Instrumental]', 'I'm Happy Just To Dance With You', 'And I Love Her [Instrumental]', 'I Should Have Known Better', 'If I Fell', 'And I Love Her', 'Ringo's Theme (This Boy) [Instrumental]', 'Can't Buy Me Love', 'A Hard Day's Night [Instrumental]'
This US variant of *A Hard Day's Night* preceded the UK version by three weeks. It includes only the eight songs from side A of the UK release, padded out by four instrumentals which are not by The Beatles.

It was released by United Artists, under licence from Capitol, over a month before the film's US premiere. This cunning marketing ploy ensured that The

Beatles had both the number one album and single the fim *A Hard Day's Night* opened on 11 August 1964.

A Hard Day's Night (UK album)

10 July 1964.
Chart position. UK: 1.
A Hard Day's Night is the only Beatles album that is solely comprised of Lennon and McCartney songs. We've already noted that, lyrically, the band's focus was moving away from direct crowd-pleasing messages to their fans (exemplified by their first five singles) to more serious, self-examining, deeper and personal themes. They're growing as writers, performers and people. It's an introspective album, and despite being recorded in two halves (the songs on side one pre-date the remainder by three months), this is a fully realised, carefully crafted statement: it's arguably their first thematic album, and not simply a collection of songs.

It also sounds great, laid down onto EMI's new Telefunken M10, first used for 'I Want To Hold Your Hand'. The vocals, in particular, are beautifully recorded, and the instruments are carefully separated in the stereo mix (available on the 2009 re-release).

Suggests Simon Philo:

> *A Hard Day's Night* represented the single most important driver for the expansion of The Beatles' constituency, cementing the band's status as global superstars in the process. It enabled The Beatles to engage a wider demographic. The panmedia project *A Hard Day's Night* – which incorporated the movie, its soundtrack album, and related artwork – was the distillation not only of all The Beatles meant at that point but much of what they would come to mean. It showcased, for example, their ability to keep several steps ahead of the game, to innovate and extend the meaning of pop, while taking their massive fan base with them on the journey.

And although the English speaking world would know The Beatles' first film and associated album as *A Hard Day's Night*, it would be given different names in different territories. In Germany and Sweden, it went under the decidedly prosaic title of *Yeah Yeah Yeah*. The Italians knew it as *All For One* [*Tutti Per Uno*], and the French as *Four Boys In The Wind* [*Quatre Garçons Dans Le Vent*]. Best of all in Brazil, you could enjoy *The Kings Of Yeah-Yeah-Yeah* [*Os Reis do Iê-Iê-Iê*].

'A Hard Day's Night' (Lennon/McCartney)

Recorded 16 April 1964. John Lennon – double-tracked lead vocals, electric and acoustic guitars; Paul McCartney – double-tracked lead vocals, backing vocals, bass; George Harrison – electric 12-string guitar; Ringo Starr – drums, bongos, cowbell; George Martin – piano.

The opening chord in 'A Hard Day's Night' was as portentous as the snare shot on Dylan's 'Like A Rolling Stone' – simultaneously tolling the end of something and heralding the start of something else.
Simon Philo, *British Invasion: The Crosscurrents Of Musical Influence* (2014)

'A Hard Day's Night' was written and recorded expressly as the band's next single and as the opening song for their first film. As such, the immediate impact was everything. Even today, sixty years on, that opening chord remains an iconic sound of the 1960s.

Outtakes show that they took some time to get the big opening chord *just right*. The final *klangg!* is a combination of two guitars, bass, piano and percussion.

In the invaluable *Songwriting Secrets Of The Beatles,* Dominic Pedler dedicates an entire chapter to these three seconds of music. 'No single sound in the history of music is as instantly recognisable as the throat-grabbing tones that herald the start of 'A Hard Day's Night',' he writes, and suggests the following instruments and voicings:

George Harrison: Rickenbacker 360/12 12-string electric guitar – Fadd9 in 1st position
John Lennon: Gibson J-160E 6-string acoustic guitar – Fadd9 in 1st position
Paul McCartney: Hofner 500/1 electric bass – D note played on the D-string, 12th fret
George Martin: Steinway Grand Piano – D chord (D2-G2-D3)
Ringo Starr: snare drum and ride cymbal

This gives a rich combination of the deep resonance of the bass and piano with the shimmering 12-string guitar, which is notoriously difficult to tune and has pairs of strings in unison and in octaves. All of this provides uneven harmonics, especially the piano, that add to the individuality of this remarkable three-second moment. Add to that the ambience of the recording studio and the compression in the mix and it's easy to understand why the exact components of this opening chord have been under scrutiny for sixty years. At least by Beatles nerds like us.

Author Ian McDonald in his seminal book *Revolution In The Head,* describes this chord as having 'a significance in Beatles lore matched only by the concluding E major of 'A Day In The Life', the two opening and closing the group's middle period of peak creativity'.

He's right.

The other key development here is John Lennon's use of a flat seventh chord (the F chord under 'and I've been *working*'). This was an uncommon move in 1964 and another example of the musician looking for new sounds. The Beatles didn't invent this chord change – 'Well All Right' by Buddy Holly uses one ('Well all right so *I'm being* foolish') – and The Beatles themselves had used it before in 'P.S. I Love You', 'Don't Bother Me', and 'All My Loving', but its appearance here is still a notably early example of a chord change that moved popular music away from the more rigid structures of rock and roll and country (and the pop of Tin Pan Alley) and into *rock*.

By the end of the year, The Who's first single 'I Can't Explain' would use this same trick ('Got a feeling *inside*, I can't explain'), followed in 1965 by 'California Girls' ('I really *dig those styles* they wear') and later into 'Purple Haze', 'Fortunate Son', 'Something' ('something in the way she *moves*'), 'Sweet Home Alabama', 'Sweet Child O' Mine', 'Nothing Else Matters', 'Hallelujah' and hundreds of others. The Who's 'My Generation' is built entirely on changes to and from the home key to a flat-VII, with added interest through a series of climbing modulations. Likewise, 'Tomorrow Never Knows' uses only an implied change to a flat-VII (the bass doesn't shift) and nothing else.

Here was a worldwide number-one single using a novel sound that would have a major influence on the music of the 1960s and beyond. It might be simplifying a complex series of developments, but if Paul McCartney brought intuitive harmonic invention to The Beatles' music, then John Lennon instinctively added the 'weird' stuff: an equilibrium epitomised in *A Hard Day's Night*.

Listening back to the song, the guitar and piano in the solo section (1.20-1.32) sound impossibly fast and have an unusual timbre. Outtakes confirm that these were recorded as an overdub at half speed, slowing down the master and allowing those tricky notes to ring brightly. When they played it for BBC radio on 14 July 1964 (the first live performance of this song) they very obviously spliced in this section from the single version. And yet George had no problems playing the section in their next BBC session three days later, nor in concert in 1964 and 1965 as heard on *Live At The Hollywood Bowl*.

To conclude, as Alan Pollack writes in his essential *Notes On…* series of articles:

> The lyrics [of 'A Hard Day's Night'] are far from epochal or even merely profound. As touched as you might allow yourself to be by the hero's profession of loving gratitude and affectation of the working-class hero, you just as easily might be made a little uneasy by his faint air of condescending chauvinism. Beyond a point, it doesn't really matter, though. Based on 'only' music and exuberant mood alone 'if necessary', the song 'A Hard Day's Night' arguably holds a place within the uppermost echelon of The Beatles' catalogue.

'I Should Have Known Better' (Lennon/McCartney)

Recorded 25–26 February 1964. John Lennon – double-tracked vocals, acoustic guitar, harmonica; Paul McCartney – bass; George Harrison – electric 12-string guitar; Ringo Starr – drums.

'I Should Have Known Better' was the first song recorded for the band's forthcoming album and film. It was written in late January. George had acquired a copy of *The Freewheelin' Bob Dylan* in Paris that month during their two-and-a-half week residency in Paris, and Dylan's influence is shown across the new album in the heft of their lyrics and the almost supernatural craft of their songwriting.

Recording sessions commenced less than a week after returning from the US. The first three takes of 'I Should Have Known Better' were left incomplete, but after making some changes to the arrangement the following day, they completed the track in another 18 takes. 'I Should Have Known Better' marks both a beginning, as the first song for a new album, and also an end: Lennon's harmonica playing. This marks the last occasion The Beatles were to feature this instrument on an introduction of a song joining a list including 'Love Me Do', 'Please Please Me' and 'From Me To You'.

It's a simple but catchy song, mostly in the easy guitar chords of G and D but with a couple of drops to Em to add colour (in the verse: 'everything that you *do*' at 0.17; in the verse: '*That* when I tell you…' at 0.40).

George plays some big chords and a brief solo in the middle section on his new Rickenbacker 12-string guitar, the first time he played it at a Beatles session ('You Can't Do That' was recorded later but released first).

The mono and stereo versions have slightly different harmonica introductions. In the stereo version, at 0.04, the harmonica drops out briefly (the mono version was released on CD and is the common streaming version, too, but the song can be heard in stereo on the *US Albums* box set). There is an audible tape edit at 2.16 during the second chorus between 'You're gonna say you love me too, oh,' and 'And when I ask you to be mine' which is more obvious in the stereo mix.

'I Should Have Known Better' is the first song performed in the film, in the famous card-playing train carriage scene (thirteen minutes in), filmed in a stationary guard's van at Twickenham Film Studios on 11 March 1964, less than two weeks after the song had been recorded. The van was rocked by members of the film crew to mimic the movements of a train.

'If I Fell' (Lennon/McCartney)

Recorded 27 February 1964. John Lennon – double-tracked vocals, acoustic guitar; Paul McCartney – double-tracked vocals, bass; George Harrison – electric 12-string guitar; Ringo Starr – drums.

'If I Fell', another very personal song, opens with an introductory section sung by John Lennon on his own and yet written by Paul McCartney. 'I was a big fan of the preamble in my early days, which you find in lots of '50s songs,' he told *Q* magazine in 2013. 'One song I wrote … was my best attempt at a preamble: 'If I Fell'. [Sings] 'If I fell in love with you, would you promise to be truuue…' Then after the line, 'just holding hands', the song properly gets going.'

'If I Fell' swoops into the verse's gorgeous two-part harmonies, recorded nose-to-nose at a single microphone, then double-tracked, with, for the most part, Paul singing the melody and John providing a low harmony. At times, they switch, and, as Dominic Pedler asserts, '[The] two independent melody lines passing like 'ships in the night', [mark] a degree of sophistication in a pop song that is light years removed from the standard 7th blues effect.'

Speaking in *Many Years From Now* about another song from later in 1964, but applying just as much here, Paul would say, 'Sometimes the harmony I was writing in sympathy to John's melody would take over and become a stronger melody. Sometimes, a piebald rabbit came out of the hat! When people wrote out the music score, they would ask, 'Which one is the melody?' because it was so co-written that you could actually take either.'

Paul's voice breaks on the 'in vain' high note at 1.45 (he'd got there earlier, at 1.09). That one moment opens up the unexpected vulnerability found in Lennon's lyrics.

These superb vocals are underpinned by intricate and fast-moving chord changes with the use of minor seventh, 9th and diminished chords, making the song tricky to play. Nevertheless, it was gamely if shakily performed live in 1964 and was introduced by John at their 2 September show in Philadelphia as 'If I Fell… Over'. The recording of this show reveals that John and Paul get a serious case of the giggles after they forget the words in the second verse.

It's still a beautiful song.

'I'm Happy Just To Dance With You' (Lennon/McCartney)

Recorded 1 March 1964. George Harrison – lead vocals, lead guitar; John Lennon – backing vocals, rhythm guitar; Paul McCartney – backing vocals, bass; Ringo Starr – drums, African drum.

'I'm Happy Just To Dance With You' was written for George.

'This one… was a straight co-written song for George,' Paul told Barry Miles. 'The ones that pandered to the fans, in truth, were our least favourite songs, but they were good. They were good for the time. The nice thing about it was to actually pull a song off on a slim little premise like that. A simple little idea. It was songwriting practice.'

It bears some similarities to 'Do You Want To Know A Secret?', sharing a key and similar chord sequences. It was recorded in four takes on a Sunday morning, the day before shooting was due to commence on the film *A Hard Day's Night*.

Listen in stereo. Lennon's busy rhythm guitar is panned far right, with the irregular thump of Ringo's drum overdubs, credited as an 'African drum' but sounding like de-tuned tom-toms. The left channel highlights the world-class McCartney-Starr rhythm section.

Years later, Canadian chanteuse Anne Murray would record this song as a slow ballad in a style not so far from The Carpenters. It's horrendous.

'And I Love Her' (Lennon/McCartney)

Recorded 25–27 February 1964. Paul McCartney – vocals, bass; John Lennon – acoustic guitar; George Harrison – classical guitar; Ringo Starr – bongos, claves.

Even if the writing on *A Hard Day's Night* is dominated by John Lennon in terms of song count, he is surely matched and exceeded by Paul in quality. 'And I Love Her' is a jewel of melody, harmony, singing and performance. The song – Paul's first 'Yesterday' as John would later concede – was written for Jane Asher. He wrote in *The Lyrics: 1956 To The Present*:

> Precisely because Jane was my girlfriend,' 'I wanted to tell her there that I loved her, so that's what initially inspired this song; that's what it was. Listening to it so many years later, I do think it's a nice melody. It starts with F-sharp minor, not with the root chord of E major, and you gradually work your way back. When I'd finished it, I felt almost immediately, proud of it. I thought, 'This is a good 'un'.

They took a few goes to get it right. The first arrangement, with Ringo's thumping toms, furiously strummed acoustics and chiming 12-string Rickenbaker, can be heard on *Anthology 2*. A more subtle approach was needed and they reworked the song the following day for classical guitars and gentle Latin percussion, and now with a short bridge ('a love like ours'). It was only on the third day that they were satisfied. The simple four-note guitar riff that underpins the introduction was suggested by George Harrison.

'We were about to record it,' McCartney wrote later, 'and [George Martin] said, 'I think it would be good with an introduction.' And I swear, right there and then, George Harrison went, 'Well how about this?' and he played the opening riff, which is such a hook; the song is nothing without it. We were working very fast and spontaneously coming up with ideas.'

George also provides a delicate counterpoint melody under the verses and a fluently beautiful guitar solo after a sly modulation up to Gm from F#m. That one half-step seems to lighten the mood of the song. The solo is impeccable – this is as much George's song as Paul's – and we close with a hum and a glorious major chord. Everything is alright in the world… and I love her.

'Tell Me Why' (Lennon/McCartney)

Recorded 27 February 1964. John Lennon – lead vocals, rhythm guitar (Lennon's vocals is double-tracked in the stereo mix, but single-tracked in the mono mix); Paul McCartney – backing vocals, bass; George Harrison – backing vocals, lead guitar; Ringo Starr – drums; George Martin – piano.

'Tell Me Why' offers an up-tempo reworking of girl-group favourites such as 'Baby It's You', using the standard *I – vi – ii – V* doo-wop chord changes heard in Lennon's beloved Smokey Robinson songs (and his own 'This Boy'). McCartney's walking bass line roots the song in the blues, but the harmonies are 100% Beatles. They up the ante with the sheer attack and urgency in their delivery.

Even if the music is 'up', the imploring lyrics are gloomily unhappy:

Well, I beg you on my bended knees
If you'll only listen to my pleas
Is there anything I can do?

'Tell Me Why' was featured in the studio performance sequence of *A Hard Day's Night,* filmed in front of 350 fans at the Scala Theatre, London, on 31 March 1964. A Google search for 'Tell Me Why' in 2025 brings up an identically-titled song by Taylor Swift. *Plus ca change ...*

'Can't Buy Me Love'
Previously released as a single.

'Any Time At All' (Lennon/McCartney)
Recorded 2 June 1964. John Lennon – lead vocals, acoustic guitar; Paul McCartney – backing vocals, bass, piano; George Harrison – electric 12-string guitar, classical guitar; Ringo Starr – drums, cowbell.
Other than the older, already-released 'You Can't Do That, side two of the original album and the rest of the *Long Tall Sally* EP was squeezed into four days of sessions at the beginning of June 1964.

1 June: 'I'll Be Back', 'I'll Cry Instead', 'Slow Down', 'Matchbox'
2 June: 'Any Time At All', 'When I Get Home'
2-3 June: 'Things We Said Today'
4 June: overdub for 'Slow Down'

These sessions were their first for three months and were dominated by John Lennon songs, starting with the huge thump on the drums that opens 'Any Time At All'. This call-to-action is similar to the earlier 'It Won't Be Long', also opening with an aggressive refrain.

John's assertive vocals in the chorus are matched by a soft, almost sensual delivery in the verses – even in a minor song such as this Lennon's commitment and vocal skills are never half-cocked. Note also that the rhymes fall on the second/fifth and third/sixth lines of the verse ('eyes'/'sympathise' and 'right'/'tonight' in the first verse, for example). There is interest in the overlapping vocal lines, Paul covering that high note in the refrain and George's twanging Rickenbacker throughout.

Writes Alan Pollack:

In terms of verbal theme, 'Any Time At All' turns out to provide an uncanny mirror image of what we saw in 'Thank You Girl'. In both songs, there is someone who offers him or herself up completely and unconditionally to support another should such help be wanted or needed. The only real difference between them is in the singer's point of view; here he is the offerer, and there he's the receiver. The common denominator of the two songs rather casually provides food for thought about just how it is that mutual love sometimes begins. John seems to imply that when you offer emotional support to another who may have never explicitly solicited it from you that this may yet turn out to be a prime movement. Read the lyrics of both songs carefully: in neither case is it necessarily true that the two people involved are aware of any mutual interest prior to the offer of support. This raises the profound question of whether love may indeed ignite based on this kind of sympathetic interest of a third party in absence of any pre-existing acquaintance or attraction.

The song itself is arguably incomplete: there are no lyrics in the sixteen-second middle eight (1.31-1,47), with Paul adding a rising figure on piano instead. There is an audible dissonance between the instruments in this section, which can only have been deliberate. The mono release of *Something New* contains an alternative mix of this instrumental bridge, which fades out the piano almost entirely.

Filler? Maybe. But top class, of course.

'I'll Cry Instead' (Lennon/McCartney)

Recorded 1 June 1964. John Lennon – double-tracked vocals, acoustic guitar; Paul McCartney – bass; George Harrison – lead guitar; Ringo Starr – drums, tambourine.

Originally submitted for the film *A Hard Day's Night* but switched in favour of 'Can't Buy Me Love', 'I'll Cry Instead' is one of Lennon's self-examinations delivered in a Dylanesque meter and blanketed in a C & W twang.

'I've got a chip on my shoulder that's bigger than my feet,' Lennon claims, once again underlining the theme of a perceived sense of insecurity that runs through several of his songs of this period. The lines 'I can't talk to people that I meet' and 'I get shy when they start to stare/I'm gonna hide myself away' are revealing insights into Lennon's psyche only one year after his band's initial successes that he finds it impossible to communicate.

The song was recorded in two sections which were edited together at 1.07 (after 'until then'). The mono release of *Something New* contains an alternative edit at this same point, which is lengthened by twenty seconds with a repeat of the first verse (it might be spliced in from a different take, but to our ears, it's a repeat from earlier in the same take).

'Things We Said Today' (Lennon/McCartney)

Recorded 2–3 June 1964. Paul McCartney – double tracked vocals, bass; John Lennon – acoustic guitar, piano; George Harrison – electric guitar; Ringo Starr – drums, tambourine.

As The Beatles matured as songwriters and performers, their new material sounded effortless. Through experimentation and intuition, they started to disregard the songwriting 'rules' learned through the performance of countless cover versions since 1956.

'Things We Said Today' displays some complex chord changes, including an unexpected, spicy move to Bb on 'Someday, when I'm lonely', which musicologist Walter Everett describes as 'Chopinesque' and elsewhere has been compared to 17th century Neapolitan opera.

Less grandly, the song was written on a cheap acoustic guitar during a boating holiday in the Virgin Islands in May 1964.

'I remember writing 'Things We Said Today' in one of the cabins below deck one afternoon,' Paul McCartney told Barry Miles in *Many Years From Now*. 'I started with an A minor chord. A minor to E minor to A minor, which gave me a sort of folksy, whimsical world. And then in the middle, on 'Me, I'm just the lucky kind', it goes to the major and gets hopeful. The thing I always loved and still love about writing a song is that, at the end of two or three hours, I have a newborn baby to show everyone. I want to show it to the world, and the world at that moment was the people on the boat.'

As Paul says, the song changes between major and minor keys, a trait that was deployed in several songs of this period, including 'And I Love Her', 'When I Get Home' and 'I'll Be Back' from *A Hard Day's Night*.

The lyrics, surely written for Jane Asher, shift between the present tense and a kind of future nostalgia ('Me, I'm just the lucky kind' and 'Then we will remember'). There are some cheeky rhymes ('luck and 'enough', 'one' and 'on').

There's also a sudden swerve to a flat chord in the verse, under 'wishing you weren't so far away', as Paul explained: 'It goes C, F, which is all normal, then the normal thing might be to go to F minor, but to go to the flat was quite good. It was a sophisticated little tune.'

Released as a B-side on the same day as the album *A Hard Day's Night*, 'Things We Said Today' comes close to outshining the more famous album-titling A-side. The group played it during their tour of North America in August-September 1964.

'When I Get Home' (Lennon/McCartney)

Recorded 2 June 1964. John Lennon – lead vocals, rhythm guitar; Paul McCartney – backing vocals, bass, piano; George Harrison – backing vocals, lead guitar; Ringo Starr – drums.

The impatient, edgy 'When I Get Home' has a real sense of urgency right from the off with harmonised 'Whoa-ah…' backing vocals and a strong Motown beat. Ringo plays neat snare fills at 0.15 and 0.44.

Trivia: The mono release of 'When I Get Home' on *Something New* has a different vocal passage from the UK mono mix. At 1.31 (or so), John's soulful lift on the word *walk* is much more effective on the US mix than the snappier UK version (which is also used on the 2009 remaster).

'You Can't Do That'

Previously released as a single B-side.

'I'll Be Back' (Lennon/McCartney)

Recorded 1 June 1964. John Lennon – double-tracked vocals, acoustic guitar; Paul McCartney – backing vocals, bass; George Harrison – backing vocals, classical guitar, acoustic guitar; Ringo Starr – drums.

'I'll Be Back' is a major song in The Beatles' oeuvre. Lennon himself admitted that it took its cue and tone from Del Shannon's 'Runaway'. Passing through similar chord changes in the verse sections, the performance and production of 'I'll Be Back' is starkly melancholic. Compare this with the out-and-out rockers that closed out the band's first two albums, namely 'Twist And Shout' and 'Money (That's What I Want)'.

As with 'I'll Cry Instead', the lyrics are vulnerable, almost confessional.

Outtakes illustrate the progression from an electric full-band waltz-time arrangement (take 2, *Anthology 1*) , through a gorgeous electric full-band 4/4 version (take 3 *Anthology 1*), to an acoustic version (takes 12-15, end credits of the *Anthology* TV series).

'I'll Be Back' combines fearless chord changes, glorious harmonies, lush nylon-strung acoustics and wry guitar embellishments, especially George's delicious four-note hook (F# – B – E – C# under an interesting chordal switch from A to Am: that major to minor tone switch was one of The Beatles' brilliant song-writing traits).

There is a guitar overdub in the opening moments (0.09-0.10 and 0.20-0.21) which, as with the piano on 'Any Time At All', is an early example of The Beatles using the recording studio as a tool, adding new instrumentation in specific points within an arrangement to enhance their basic guitar/bass/drums/vocals lineup.

The way the song flows is also noteworthy:

0.00-0.04 introduction
0.04-0.27 verse 1
0.27-0.40 bridge 1
0.40-1.03 verse 2
1.03-1.22 bridge 2 (different chords than bridge 1)
1.22-1.44 verse 3 (which is repeat of verse 2)
1.44-1.58 bridge 3 (same chords as bridge 1)
1.58-2.07 verse 4 (in fact, the first half of verse 1)
2.07-2.18 fade out.

This restlessness suggests that despite the intent inherent in the opening verse, the narrator is, in fact, kidding himself about coming back at all.

All of this fantastic invention and execution, and the song's not even two-and-a-half minutes long.

'A Hard Day's Night' b/w **'Things We Said Today'** (UK single)
'A Hard Day's Night' b/w **'I Should Have Known Better'** (US single)
10 July 1964.
Chart position. UK: 1.
13 July 1964.
Chart position. UK: 1.

Something New (US album)
20 July 1964.
Chart position. US: 2.
'I'll Cry Instead', 'Things We Said Today', 'Any Time At All', 'When I Get Home', 'Slow Down', 'Matchbox', 'Tell Me Why', 'And I Love Her', 'I'm Happy Just To Dance With You', 'If I Fell', 'Komm, Gib Mir Deine Hand'
Something New duplicates five songs from the United Artists' release of *A Hard Day's Night* which came out just three weeks beforehand. Hardly something new.

Nevertheless, for Beatles completists, the mono version of this album contains mix variants of 'Any Time At All', 'I'll Cry Instead', 'When I Get Home', 'If I Fell' and 'And I Love Her' which are unique to this release.

'I'll Cry Instead' b/w **'I'm Happy Just To Dance With You'** (US single)
20 July 1964
Chart position. US: 25

'And I Love Her' b/w **'If I Fell'** (US single)
20 July 1964
Chart position. US: 12

'Matchbox' b/w **'Slow Down'** (US single)
24 August 1964
Chart position. US: 17

Extracts From The Film A Hard Day's Night EP (UK)
4 November 1964.
Chart position. UK: 1.
'I Should Have Known Better', 'If I Fell', 'Tell Me Why', 'And I Love Her'

Extracts From The Album A Hard Day's Night EP (UK)
6 November 1964.
Chart position. UK: 8.
'Any Time at All', 'I'll Cry Instead', 'Things We Said Today', 'When I Get Home'

The Beatles' Story (US album)
23 November 1964.
Chart position. US: 7.
'On Stage with the Beatles', 'How Beatlemania Began', 'Beatlemania in Action', 'Man Behind the Beatles – Brian Epstein', 'John Lennon', 'Who's a Millionaire?', 'Beatles Will Be Beatles', 'Man Behind the Music – George Martin', 'George Harrison', 'A Hard Day's Night – Their First Movie', 'Paul McCartney', 'Sneaky Haircuts and More About Paul', 'The Beatles Look at Life', 'Victims' of Beatlemania', 'Beatle Medley', 'Ringo Starr', 'Liverpool and All the World!'
Capitol recorded The Beatles' concert at the Hollywood Bowl on 23 August 1964 with the intention of releasing a live album. The band and George Martin judged it to be of poor quality, and blocked its release. In its place, Capitol pulled together this hour-long audio documentary from interviews and press conferences, snippets of hits, syrupy versions of Beatles music by The Hollywood Strings and a hilariously earnest voice-over commentary ('It started in Liverpool, a poor British seaport slum town…'). It contains a 48-second excerpt of 'Twist and Shout' from the Hollywood Bowl performance as part of the track 'The Beatles Look At Life'. This was the only availability of this live recording until 1977, when *Live At The Hollywood Bowl*, comprising recordings from 1964 and 1965, would finally be released.

'I Feel Fine' b/w **'She's A Woman'** (Single)
UK: 27 November 1964. US: 23 November 1964.
Chart positions. UK: 1. US: 1.
'Every Little Thing' (recorded 30 September) and 'Eight Days A Week' (6 October) were both candidates for The Beatles' third single of 1964, or tenth if you were an American fan. When John Lennon brought 'I Feel Fine' to the band in mid-October 1964 during the last sessions for *Beatles For Sale,* it became the de facto choice.

The musical innovations continued in the first six seconds …

'I Feel Fine' (Lennon/McCartney)
Recorded 18 October 1964. John Lennon – double-tracked lead vocals, lead and rhythm guitar; Paul McCartney – backing vocals, bass; George Harrison – backing vocals, lead guitar; Ringo Starr – drums.
'I Feel Fine' opens with a buzz of feedback from John's Gibson J-160E acoustic guitar. This was no accident – it was included in every take.
John Lennon to *Playboy*'s David Sheff in 1980:

> I defy anybody to find a record – unless it's some old blues record in 1922 – that uses feedback that way. I mean, everybody played with feedback on stage, and the Jimi Hendrix stuff was going on long before. I claim it for The

Above: Tea and history, 1965. (*Alamy*)

Left: The Beatles' manager, Brian Epstein. In his memoirs, Epstein wrote: 'I immediately liked what I heard. They were fresh, and they were honest, and they had what I thought was a sort of presence. I was … struck by their music, their beat and their sense of humour on stage – and, even afterwards, when I met them, I was struck again by their personal charm. And it was there that, really, it all started.'

Right: *Revolver* has everything. The Beatles' most varied album to that point. (*Parlophone*)

Left: After 60 years, this album still sounds like the future of popular music. (*Parlophone*)

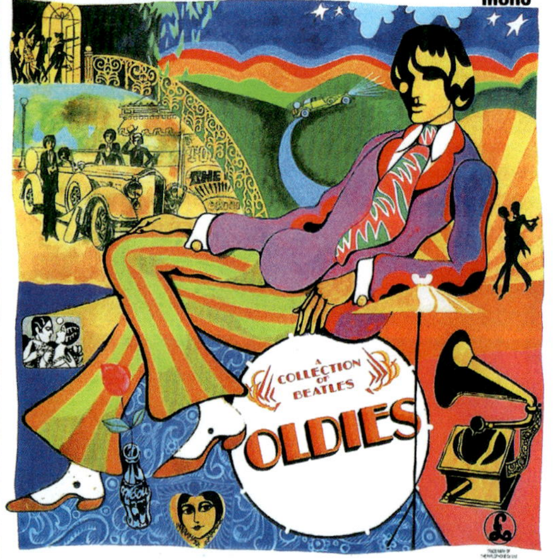

Right: The only official hits collection whilst the Beatles were still together includes the first UK release of 'Bad Boy', as well as 'Michelle' instead of either 'Love Me Do' or 'Please Please Me'. (*Parlophone*)

Left and below: *Rubber Soul*. One of the best albums by anyone, ever. (*Parlophone*)

Left: *The Beatles Million Sellers* compilation, released in the UK. Four numbers ones for 11 'bob'. (*Parlophone*)

Right: *Beatles VI* is a mish-mash of tracks from *Beatles For Sale* and *Help!*, a B-side and a track called 'Bad Boy' recorded expressly for the US market. (*Capitol*)

BEATLES VI

THE WORLD'S MOST POPULAR FOURSOME! JOHN·PAUL·GEORGE·RINGO

YOU LIKE ME TOO MUCH · TELL ME WHAT YOU SEE · BAD BOY · DIZZY MISS LIZZIE · EIGHT DAYS A WEEK · YES IT IS
WORDS OF LOVE · KANSAS CITY · I DON'T WANT TO SPOIL THE PARTY · EVERY LITTLE THING · WHAT YOU'RE DOING

RECORDED IN ENGLAND

Capitol

THE BEATLES stereo

HELP!

Left: By 1965, The Beatles were unstoppable – *Help!* set a new high point for pop albums. (*Parlophone*)

(NEW IMPROVED FULL DIMENSIONAL STEREO)

ORIGINAL MOTION PICTURE SOUNDTRACK

THE BEATLES

Capitol

HELP!

HELP! · THE NIGHT BEFORE · YOU'VE GOT TO HIDE YOUR LOVE AWAY · I NEED YOU
ANOTHER GIRL · TICKET TO RIDE · YOU'RE GONNA LOSE THAT GIRL
And Exclusive Instrumental Music From the Picture's Soundtrack

Right: The US variant of *Help!* includes only the first eight songs from the UK edition, along with a series of instrumentals taken from the film soundtrack which are not by The Beatles. (*Capitol*)

Left: One of just two EPs created for the American market. This one is from February 1965. (*Capitol*)

Right: *The Early Beatles* (1965) is yet another re-package of *Please Please Me*. (*Capitol*)

Left: The second EP of tracks from *Beatles For Sale*: 'I'll Follow The Sun', 'Baby's In Black', 'Words Of Love', 'I Don't Want To Spoil The Party'. (*Parlophone*)

Right: The collarless Pierre Cardin suits on show here in early 1964. (*Alamy*)

Above: The Beatles posing with bottles of beer and balloons in October 1964 to promote the BBC World Service. (*Mark and Colleen Hayward/Redferns*)

Above: A publicity shot from *A Hard Day's Night*. George's future wife Patti Boyd teases his mop top. (*Alamy*)

Below: A classic image of the Beatles in April 1964 during the filming of *A Hard Day's Night*. (*Alamy*)

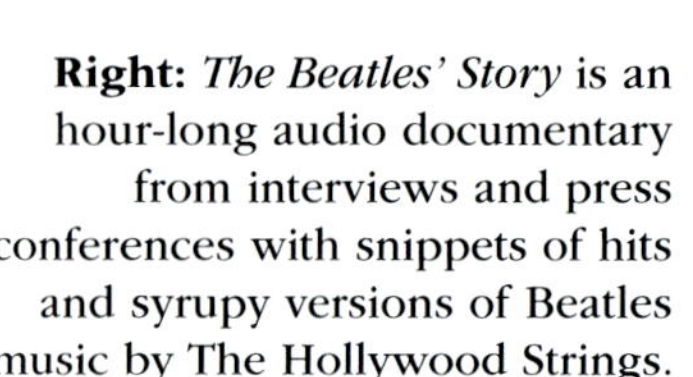

Right: *The Beatles' Story* is an hour-long audio documentary from interviews and press conferences with snippets of hits and syrupy versions of Beatles music by The Hollywood Strings. (*Capitol*)

Left: *Beatles For Sale* was the band's fourth album in 22 months. Whereas we can trace further development of their key styles, we can also see a band getting stretched by the demands of their marketplace. (*Parlophone*)

Right: *Beatles '65* is the American version of *Beatles For Sale*, with six songs removed and both sides of the recent single added, reducing the running time to just 26 minutes. (*Capitol*)

Left: *Something New* duplicates five songs from the United Artists release of *A Hard Day's Night*, released just three weeks beforehand. Hardly something new. (*Capitol*)

Right and below: These twin EPs highlight eight songs from their parent album. (*Parlophone*)

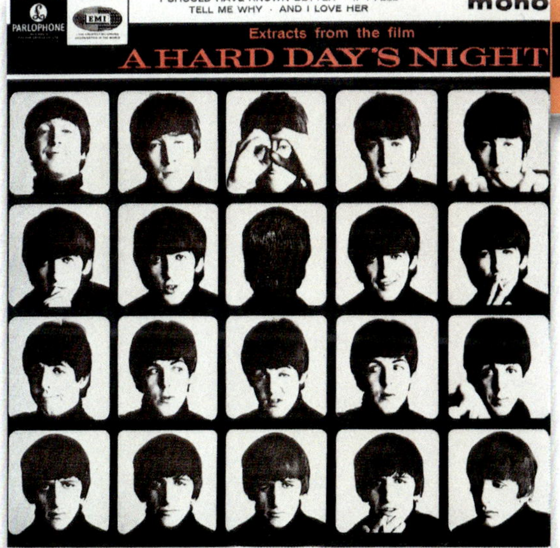

Above: *The Ed Sullivan Show* appearance in February 1964 was a major breakthrough for The Beatles, seen here with their host. (*Alamy*)

Left: The Beatles on Dutch TV on 5 June 1964. (*Alamy*)

Above: The four most famous men in the world in 1964.

Below: The Beatles with their producer George Martin. (*Alamy*)

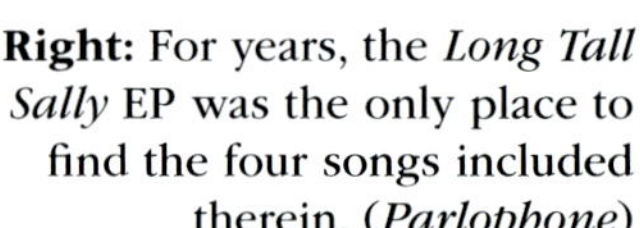

Right: For years, the *Long Tall Sally* EP was the only place to find the four songs included therein. (*Parlophone*)

Left: *A Hard Day's Night* is the only Beatles album solely comprised of Lennon and McCartney songs. They're growing, as writers, performers and people. (*Parlophone*)

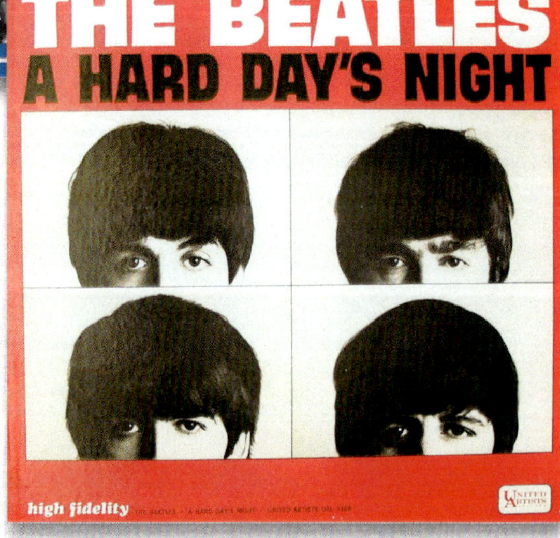

Right: This US variant of *A Hard Day's Night* preceded the UK version by three weeks. It includes only the eight songs from side A of the UK release, padded out by four instrumentals which are not by The Beatles. (*United Artists*)

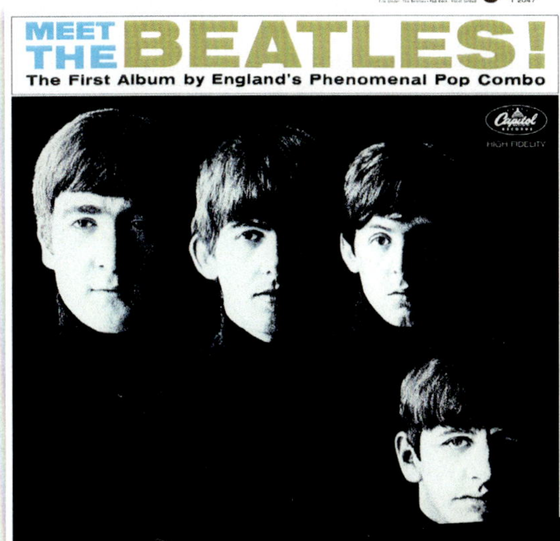

Left: *Meet The Beatles* offered only ten of the 14 songs on *With The Beatles*, plus both sides of the breakthrough single. (*Capitol*)

Right: Vee-Jay capitalised on their good fortune by re-releasing the tracks from *Please Please Me* in many guises. (*Vee-Jay*)

Left: Two months after *Meet The Beatles*, *The Beatles' Second Album* (for Capitol, at least) was a mixture of album tracks, B-sides and songs from a British EP. (*Capitol*)

Right and below: Two further EPs collected album tracks and repromoted old singles. (*Parlophone*)

Right: The first US album, *Introducing... The Beatles*, was released a week before *Meet The Beatles* in January 1964. (*Vee-Jay*)

Left: As a vehicle for showcasing The Beatles' musical skills and individual personalities, *Please Please Me* remains a superb achievement for a young band with limited studio experience. (*Parlophone*)

Right: The *Twist And Shout* EP was released in 1963 for buyers who couldn't afford to buy an LP. This was a big seller. (*Parlophone*)

Left: If *Please Please Me* was recorded, for the most part, in a single day, sessions for its follow-up, *With The Beatles*, were squeezed in between their multitude of other commitments across three months in summer and autumn 1963. (*Parlophone*)

Above: The Beatles – a cultural phenomenon like no other. (*Alamy*)

Beatles. Before Hendrix, before The Who, before anybody. The first feedback on any record.

The feedback switches to a tricky arpeggiated guitar riff that John had been messing with during sessions for 'Eight Days A Week', recorded on 6 October. That riff, muddy and gritty on John's amplified acoustic, owes a huge debt to Bobby Parker's 'Watch Your Step', as admitted by both Paul and George. It's very obvious if you listen to Parker's original. Parker himself likely lifted his guitar line from Dizzy Gillespie's 'Manteca', and Led Zeppelin reused it, note-for-note, in 'Moby Dick'.

Riff in place, Lennon wrote a song to fit around it, probably during the first seven dates of The Beatles' autumn tour of the UK and possibly even the day before the recording session when he had no other professional engagements. The Beatles returned to EMI between concerts in Hull (16 October) and Edinburgh (19 October), to finish 'Eight Days A Week', 're-record 'Mr Moonlight', lay down several cover versions (4 songs in a total of 6 takes) and, from start to finish, record both 'I'll Follow The Sun' and their next single. These guys worked hard.

'I Feel Fine' betrays none of the angst of much of Lennon's material from 1964 on *A Hard Day's Night* and the already-recorded, yet-to-be-released *Beatles For Sale*.

'I Feel Fine' mixes John's bluesy riff with a country and western feel in the vocals and Latin-styled percussion. It's irresistible. The intro adds instrumentation in layers – John's riff starts at 0.06, drums and bass and second guitar at 0.13, and vocals at 0.17. For the first time, the backing track was recorded first, and the vocals were added later. This might be responsible for the ragged timing at the end of the second verse (at 0.44).

The bridge ('I'm so glad') is straightforward beat music and leads to a wonderful eight-second guitar break (1.08-1.16) with George overdubbing a delightful counterpoint to his doubling of John's riff. Ringo's drum patterns mix 'Watch Your Step' with the Latin lope of 'What'd I Say'. There's nothing new under the sun, but Ringo's playing is joyous: he has the groove in his DNA.

'I Feel Fine' was a big seller, shipping over a million copies in both the UK and the US. At the latest count, 'I Feel Fine' was still the 53rd best-selling single of all time in the UK – The Beatles' fourth highest entry.

It was a regular in their set throughout 1965. Lennon would play that riff without looking at his hands and simultaneously singing. You try it.

'She's A Woman' (Lennon/McCartney)

Recorded 8 October 1964. Paul McCartney – double-tracked vocals, bass, piano; John Lennon – rhythm guitar; George Harrison – double-tracked lead guitar; Ringo Starr – drums, chocalho.

The bluesy feeling of 'I Feel Fine' is matched by 'She's A Woman', the first exclusive B-side since 'This Boy' a year before. Written by Paul, mostly on the day of recording it, sections of the song follow the standard twelve-bar changes, but with an introduction on the off-beat which threw them a few times during the recording sessions and still has the power to fool you even now. There's also a neat internal rhyme when Paul follows 'jealous' with 'well as'. We'll forgive the terrible 'peasant'/'present' rhyme.

The bass is mixed high: prominent and fluid.

That The Beatles enjoyed playing 'She's A Woman' is evident in a six-minute take 6, where they jam away happily.

George added two lead guitar parts in later that evening, entering at 1.53. At the same time, Ringo shook a chocalho (especially noticeable 0.14-0.15 and 0.41-0.42) and Paul overdubbed piano (entering at 0.43). Ringo is, of course, awesome.

It's Paul's song through and through and was added to the band's setlist in spring 1965. It stayed there for the next year and a half until the end of their final tour, usually performed as the second song of the set.

Beatles For Sale (UK album)

4 December 1964.
Chart position. UK: 1.

Beatles For Sale was the band's fourth album in twenty-two months, and whereas we can trace further development of their key styles (with added emphasis on acoustic guitars and C&W in places), we can also see a band getting stretched by the demands of their marketplace. There are six cover versions included on the album and eight fabulous, sometimes overlooked, Lennon/McCartney originals.

Lennon's songs carry over the themes of self-isolation from 'I'll Cry Instead' and 'I'll Be Back' on *A Hard Day's Night*. Listening now, 'I'm A Loser', 'I Don't Want To Spoil The Party' and 'No Reply' are remarkably frank in their lyrical messages. Paul's songs, without resorting to thumbs-aloft lazy observations, are upbeat and open, including the US number one single, 'Eight Days A Week', the bright 'Every Little Thing', the breezy 'I'll Follow The Sun' and the lost classic 'What You're Doing'. Whilst *Beatles For Sale* might never sit in The Beatles' top 10 albums – indeed, some critics have described it as 'uninspired and bland' – the band's Liverpool contemporaries, such as Gerry And The Pacemakers (whose hits were starting to dry up) would no doubt have loved to work with material of this calibre.

We like to think of *Beatles For Sale* as a musical 'watershed', a turning point, a pivot. After this, 1965 beckons.

'No Reply' (Lennon/McCartney)

Recorded 30 September 1964. John Lennon – double-tracked lead vocals, acoustic guitar, handclaps; Paul McCartney – backing vocals, bass, handclaps; George Harrison – acoustic guitar, electric guitar, handclaps; Ringo Starr – drums, handclaps; George Martin – piano.

'No Reply' is a low-key opening to the album, seemingly carrying on its tone and feeling directly from 'I'll Be Back'. It was written in the same time period, and was demoed at EMI on 3 June. It was offered to NEMS singer Tommy Quickly, who passed on an exclusive Lennon original. When The Beatles needed material to complete *Beatles For Sale*, they returned to 'No Reply'.

In a 1980 interview with David Sheff, Lennon said that the lyrics were inspired by 'Silhouettes', a 1957 song by The Rays. 'I had that image of walking down the street and seeing her silhouetted in the window and not answering the phone…'

Compare John's 'This happened once before when I came to your door, no reply/They said it wasn't you, but I saw you peep through your window' with the opening lines of 'Silhouettes' written by Bob Crewe and Frank Slay, Jr.: 'Took a walk and passed your house late last night/All the shades were pulled and drawn way down tight…'

The bossa nova rhythm colours some unusual chord voicings, with F6, C6, a gorgeous G6 under 'I looked up to see' (at 0.27). Tension builds with 'I saw the light' and 'I nearly died' with cymbal crashes syncopated slightly ahead of the beat, and in the latter, underpinned by George Martin's heavily reverbed piano chords.

The song bursts into life in the middle sixteen ('if I were you'), beefed up by a straight-beat rhythm, handclaps and soaring harmonies. This astonishing thirty-second section appears just once in the song: a diamond that is shared, but only briefly.

There is an outrageous C6add9 chord to close the song.

The self-examination and downbeat mood of 'No Reply' continue with the next two songs on the album.

'I'm A Loser' (Lennon/McCartney)

Recorded 14 August 1964. John Lennon – lead vocals, harmonica, acoustic guitar; Paul McCartney – backing vocals, bass; George Harrison – lead guitar; Ringo Starr – drums, tambourine.

'I'm A Loser' has strong hints of Bob Dylan – Zimmerman with a punch – and anticipates the soon-to-explode folk-rock movement of the following spring. The acoustic timbres of 'I'll Be Back' and 'Things We Said Today' from earlier in 1964 also provided further subtle nods to Dylan and the emerging folk movement. These would become more obvious in 'You've Got To Hide Your Love Away' and 'Norwegian Wood (This Bird Has Flown)' in 1965.

Compare also 'Although I laugh and I act like a clown/beneath this mask I am wearing a frown' with 'I heard the sound of a clown who cried in the alley' from Dylan's 'A Hard Rain's A-Gonna Fall'.

The musical arrangement leans on county music with twanging guitar. Compare George's finger-pinking on 'I'm A Loser' with Buck Owens' 'Act Naturally' and their own 'What Goes On' both recorded the following year. There's also a delicious walking bass line under the chorus.

The bootleg album *Minus One* includes the basic take of 'I'm A Loser'. Lennon's dry, single-tracked vocals are shockingly forthright when not buried in overdubs and swallowed by reverb. Listen out for an uncharacteristic low G, most obvious at 0.53, and the Dylan-inspired harmonica solos (1.15-1.26 and 2.09-2.20), the last time this instrument was used as a solo embellishment within a Beatles song.

'Baby's In Black' (Lennon/McCartney)

Recorded 11 August 1964. John Lennon – vocals, acoustic guitar; Paul McCartney – vocals, bass; George Harrison – lead guitar; Ringo Starr – drums, tambourine.

The two glum opening tracks from *Beatles For Sale* are joined by a third, a straight Lennon and McCartney co-composition. 'Baby's In Black' sounds like The Crickets or The Everly Brothers singing an intense blues waltz. Paul and John are in tight harmony, recorded at a single microphone (like 'If I Fell') during the first session for the album.

Paul in *Anthology*: "Baby's In Black' we did because we like waltz time – we used to do 'If You Gotta Make A Fool Of Somebody', a cool 3/4 blues thing. And other bands would notice that and say, 'Shit man, you're doing something in 3/4.' So we'd got known for that. And I think also John and I wanted to do something bluesy, a bit darker, more grown-up, rather than just straight pop. It was more 'baby's in black' as in mourning. Our favourite colour was black, as well.'

George's short but marvellous guitar solo is dissonant, full of bent notes and wry invention. There is a very noticeable mistake at 1.45 when Paul sings 'and so', and John sings 'but so'.

The Beatles were fond enough to add 'Baby's In Black' to their setlist for their Christmas 1964 shows at the Hammersmith Odeon. It stayed there for the next 20 months, for Shea Stadium, Hollywood Bowl and through to the last concert of all on 29 August 1966.

'Rock And Roll Music' (Berry)

Recorded 18 October 1964. John Lennon – vocals, rhythm guitar, piano; Paul McCartney – bass, piano; George Harrison – lead guitar; Ringo Starr – drums; George Martin – piano.

Short of original songs, 'Rock And Roll Music' was one of five cover versions and two original songs recorded in a single day to fill out *Beatles For Sale* and the band's next single. It's a spirited, if perfunctory run-through of a Chuck Berry song that had been in the band's set list since 1959.

John gives it some welly, with a committed vocal (hear him run out of breath at 0.36) and a hard-rocking one-take arrangement which has Ringo's solid, rocking drums. This is in direct contrast to Chuck Berry's more laid-back original.

George Martin is credited on piano, but it sounds like Paul to us. Ringo drops in a neat Latin beat under the final bridge.

The intense vocals and a tough groove add up to give us a really nice cover version. In some countries, 'Rock And Roll Music' was released as a single in early 1965 with 'I'm A Loser' as the B-side. It topped the charts in Norway, Sweden, Finland and Australia and was top three in Germany, the Netherlands and Belgium.

For their 1966 tour they would open their concerts with 'Rock And Roll Music'. By then, they were going through the motions. It seems unlikely that John would have approved release of the painful version recorded in Tokyo and heard on *Anthology 2*.

'I'll Follow The Sun' (Lennon/McCartney)

Recorded 18 October 1964. Paul McCartney – lead and backing vocals, acoustic guitar; John Lennon – backing vocals; George Harrison – electric guitar; Ringo Starr – percussion.

The main melody of 'I'll Follow The Sun' dates back to 1958. It was first recorded in 1960 when the band borrowed a portable reel-to-reel. Even then, in this early version, it's a pretty tune, and harmonically complex – very advanced for a sixteen-year-old composer. It seems to speak about unrequited love and the need to let go.

When they needed new songs for *Beatles For Sale*, 'I'll Follow The Sun' was dusted down and refreshed, with a neater introduction and sweeter melody. Paul and John wrote a new middle eight ('and now the time has come') replacing a weak instrumental section in the previous arrangement.

The song is so beautiful and well-constructed that it's difficult to believe that McCartney had no musical training whatsoever.

'I'll Follow The Sun' was laid down at EMI in eight takes. Paul sings and plays, for the first time on a Beatles song, acoustic guitar, including that tricky finger-picked introduction. Here is another example of The Beatles thinking about different sound palettes and different ways of recording. John sings harmony and some delicate supporting singing under the first few lines of each verse. George's adds beautifully warm electric guitar and Ringo taps his knees. Wonderful.

'Mr Moonlight' (Johnson)

Recorded 18 October 1964. John Lennon – vocals, rhythm guitar; Paul McCartney – backing vocals, bass, Hammond organ; George Harrison – backing vocals, lead guitar, African drum; Ringo Starr – conga.

Another song from the marathon session of 18 October. An earlier 14 August version, the same day as the outstanding outtake 'Leave My Kitten Alone', was deemed unsuitable.

This is a cover of a B-side by Dr Feelgood And The Interns, first released in January 1962. The group name was a cover-all for Willie Lee 'Piano Red' Perryman and his band. In this case. 'Mr Moonlight' was written and sung by the band's guitarist, Roy Lee Johnson.

Rearranged by The Beatles for beat combo and often used as an attention-grabbing set-opener. John's gritty, full-throated opening note is astounding. A ripping version can heard on the Star-Club album. An early studio take is included on *Anthology 1*.

The remake is cheesy enough to be sold at a supermarket. John's good, though.

Two other Northern beat groups recorded 'Mr. Moonlight' before The Beatles. It's the second track on The Hollies' *Stay With The Hollies*, recorded at Abbey Road in December 1963 and released the following month. The Merseybeats recorded a faithful cover of the original as the B-side of their top five single 'I Think Of You', a hit in spring 1964. Neither of these are particularly ground-breaking. The Beatles' version includes the first example of any of the band playing an electronic keyboard: Paul's thrumming Hammond organ. You can visualise his joy when playing the deliberately naff solo.

It's almost impossible to draw a line from 'Mr Moonlight' to 'A Day In The Life', recorded just over two years later.

'Kansas City/Hey-Hey-Hey-Hey!' (Leiber-Stoller/Penniman)

Recorded 18 October 1964. Paul McCartney – lead vocals, bass; John Lennon – backing vocals, rhythm guitar; George Harrison – backing vocals, lead guitar; Ringo Starr – drums; George Martin – piano.

Paul sings Little Richard's medley of two of his songs, first recorded in 1955 and 1956 and recorded in this arrangement in 1958 on *The Fabulous Little Richard* and, the following spring, as a single.

It was introduced to The Beatles' set in 1960. Bootleg recordings from The Cavern (September 1962, thrilling) and Hamburg (December 1962) exist, as well as four different versions for the BBC in 1963 and 1964.

The Beatles had performed in Kansas City, Missouri, on 17 September 1964, where they were paid $150,000 for a 32-minute show. This medley was dropped into a set that also included 'Twist And Shout', 'You Can't Do That', 'All My Loving', 'She Loves You', 'Things We Said Today', 'Roll Over Beethoven', 'Can't Buy Me Love', 'If I Fell', 'I Want To Hold Your Hand', 'Boys', 'A Hard Day's Night', and 'Long Tall Sally'.

Four weeks later, it was recorded at EMI. It does its job: loud and brash, with Paul at full throttle.

'Eight Days A Week' (Lennon/McCartney)

Recorded 6 and 18 October 1964. John Lennon – vocals, acoustic guitar, handclaps; Paul McCartney – vocals, bass, handclaps; George Harrison – backing vocals, lead guitars, handclaps; Ringo Starr – drums, handclaps.

A stone-cold classic, the majority of 'Eight Days A Week' was recorded on 6 October 1964, potentially as a single. Capitol realised this and held it back from *Beatles '65* for single release the following February. It was their seventh number-one single in the US.

'By the time we came to the session,' Paul is quoted in *The Lyrics: 1956 To The Present*, ' John and I could play it on acoustic guitars for George, Ringo, George Martin, and the engineer. None of them had ever heard it before. John and I were the only two who knew it, but within twenty minutes, we'd all learnt it.'

There are some innovations here. The atmospheric fade-in was a first, with several ideas being tried until they settled on the chiming guitars. Extracts from takes one, two and four from the 6 October session were included on *Anthology 1*, along with the complete take five. The angular bridge has an unusual feel, especially Paul's incredible high harmony that includes a melisma (on 'I lo-o-o-o-o-ve you' at 1.06) not at all common in pop music in 1964. This adds an Eastern, almost Indian vibe. And to contrast with that unusual fade-in there is a complete ending.

During the 6 October session, John is playing around with a guitar riff that would develop into 'I Feel Fine', recorded twelve days later.

'Words Of Love' (Holly)

Recorded 18 October 1964. John Lennon – lead vocals, rhythm guitar; Paul McCartney – lead vocals, bass; George Harrison – backing vocals, double-tracked lead guitar; Ringo Starr – drums, packing case.

Buddy Holly gave The Beatles their name and ten early covers, and here is the only EMI version of one of his songs (there were several more recorded for the BBC). 'Words Of Love' is a lovely tribute to one of The Beatles' biggest influences, the last of the seven songs recorded in a single day to meet the album's deadline.

Paul, to *Disc*, 14 November 1964: 'This isn't ours. It's an old Buddy Holly speciality which we used to do again at The Cavern. There was a fabulous guitar bit on the Holly disc, sounding almost like bells. George took the same riff and double-tracked it, and sounds just as good.'

This can be heard at 0.57 in Holly's original and from 1.00 to 1.19 in The Beatles' cover.

Listen to the singing. Is it John and Paul? Paul and George? John and George? All three?

'Honey Don't' (Perkins)

Recorded 26 October 1964. Ringo Starr – lead vocals, drums, percussion; John Lennon – acoustic guitar; Paul McCartney – bass; George Harrison – lead guitar.

It's definitely Ringo singing Carl Perkins once again – 'Honey Don't' is much more acceptable than 'Matchbox' from a few months earlier. It was the B-side of Perkins' 'Blue Suede Shoes' (1957) and had been sung by John since 1962.

It's ideal for Ringo's laid-back charm, full of character and absolutely the right song choice. He seemingly suppresses laughter in the first chorus at 0.34. He says 'I feel fine' at 1.30, The Beatles' next single recorded the previous week.

'Every Little Thing' (Lennon/McCartney)
Recorded 30 September 1964. John Lennon – double-tracked lead vocals, acoustic guitar; Paul McCartney – backing vocals, bass, piano; George Harrison – double-tracked lead guitar; Ringo Starr – drums, timpani.
Tucked away at the back of *Beatles For Sale* are three overlooked and excellent original songs, 'Every Little Thing', 'I Don't Want To Spoil The Party' and 'What You're Doing'. These were recorded across two days of sessions, 29-30 September 1964, although one was later remade.

The very appealing, occasionally melodramatic and emotionally revealing 'Every Little Thing' was (mostly) written by Paul for Jane Asher and is (mostly) sung by John. 'The opening couplet,' writes Alan Pollack in his *Notes On* series, 'resonates with earlier examples of John's preoccupation with factoring in the opinions of un-named others when it comes to his taking the measure of his sense of self-satisfaction or self-worth when it comes to affairs of the heart.'

As if to underpin this, there is a delightful piano counter-melody in the verses, first heard at 0.10. Ringo bongs timpani at 0.31 during the infectious chorus, another example of instrumentation outside the standard guitar-bass-drums beat combo. Paul adds resonating piano here, too.

Perhaps surprisingly, proggers Yes covered 'Every Little Thing' on their self-titled debut album (1969). Their arrangement adds a two-minute heavy introduction, snippets of 'Day Tripper', dynamic verses and some clever harmonic touches.

'I Don't Want To Spoil The Party' (Lennon/McCartney)
Recorded 29 September 1964. John Lennon – lead vocals, acoustic guitar; Paul McCartney – bass, backing vocals; George Harrison – lead guitar, backing vocals; Ringo Starr – drums, tambourine.
'I Don't Want To Spoil The Party' is a very personal, melancholic, sometimes ambiguous John Lennon song. The last of nineteen takes was included on *Beatles For Sale*. The narrator – we assume it's John – has been stood up at a social gathering. Expressing a fear of abandonment and in a bad mood, he extricates himself. There's a notable mention of alcohol ('I've had a drink or two, and I don't care'): the first in a Beatles original, after 'A Taste Of Honey' (wine) and 'Rock And Roll Music' (homebrew).

The arrangement of 'I Don't Want To Spoil The Party' leans towards C & W, dominated by John's acoustic guitar and punctuated by George's best Carl Perkins licks on his new Gretsch Tennessean.

The wordless backing vocals in the verses are rich, and in the bridge, they are particularly robust with a bracing open fifth on the word 'love' (first heard at 0.56).

'What You're Doing' (Lennon/McCartney)
Recorded 26 October 1964. Paul McCartney – lead vocals, bass; John Lennon – backing vocals, acoustic guitar; George Harrison – backing vocals, 12-string electric guitar; Ringo Starr – drums; George Martin – piano.

First recorded on 29 September, this early version is one of the great unreleased outtakes. There are some smart internal rhymes ('doing'/'blue and'; 'running'/'fun in') that are no doubt influenced by Bob Dylan and recycled from the earlier 'She's A Woman'.

The remake from four weeks later is sharper, if not as immediate. It borrows its opening drum pattern directly from The Supremes' 'Be My Baby' (go and listen to it, the resemblance is uncanny). George plays his Rickenbaker 12-string and there is some distortion on the guitar solo (1.21-1.35). The bass is mixed loudly, and the backing vocals are very carefully arranged, accenting certain words and phrases anticipating a trick used to great effect in rap and hip hop many years later (before you write in, we are not suggesting The Beatles invented hip-hop… but track down Danger Mouse's *The Grey Album* which mashes The Beatles with Jay-Z).

In these small sonic touches we are seeing progress from early to mid-stage Beatles.

Finally, does 'What You're Doing' offer early proof of Paul's use of pot? The arrangement and texture is, to coin a phrase, laid back, and the lyrics are angrily sarcastic: 'Would it be too much to ask of you/What you're doing to me?'

'Everybody's Trying To Be My Baby' (Perkins)

Recorded 18 October 1964. George Harrison – double-tracked lead vocals, lead guitar; John Lennon – acoustic guitar, tambourine; Paul McCartney – bass; Ringo Starr – drums.

George sings Carl Perkins, drenched in STEED echo. It sounds like he's singing in a bathroom at the end of the hall.

The band had recorded this song twice for the BBC in 1963-1964 and now here, in a single take, for EMI. George's playing is precise and stylish (two solos!), even if his thick accent dominates the double-tracked vocals.

It was added to The Beatles' set for 1965.

Beatles '65 (US album)

15 December 1964.

Chart position. US: 1.

'No Reply', 'I'm A Loser', 'Baby's In Black', 'Rock And Roll Music', 'I'll Follow The Sun', 'Mr. Moonlight', 'Honey Don't', 'I'll Be Back', 'She's A Woman', 'I Feel Fine', 'Everybody's Trying To Be My Baby'

Beatles '65 is the American version of *Beatles For Sale,* with six songs removed and both sides of the recent single added, reducing the running time to just 26 minutes.

As the first new Beatles album for five months, it was hugely popular: number one for nine weeks and the biggest-selling pop album of 1965.

1965

4 By The Beatles EP (US)
1 February 1965.
Chart position. US: 68.
'Honey Don't', 'I'm A Loser', 'Mr. Moonlight', 'Everybody's Trying To Be My Baby'

'Eight Days A Week' b/w **'I Don't Want To Spoil The Party'** (US single)
15 February 1965.
Chart positions. US: 1.

The Early Beatles (US album)
22 March 1965.
Chart position. US: 43.
'Love Me Do', 'Twist and Shout', 'Anna (Go to Him)', 'Chains', 'Boys', 'Ask Me Why', 'Please Please Me', 'P.S. I Love You', 'Baby It's You', 'A Taste of Honey', 'Do You Want to Know a Secret'
With Capitol not interested in The Beatles in 1963, EMI had licenced the songs from the *Please Please Me* album to Vee Jay Records. When that arrangement ended, Capitol were able to release the songs themselves on an album called *The Early Beatles*. Or most of them: 'I Saw Her Standing There' had appeared on Meet The Beatles!, which is fair enough, but – inexplicably – both 'Misery' and 'There's A Place' were omitted. They were not available on a Capitol album until 1980's *Rarities*.

Beatles For Sale EP (UK)
6 April 1965.
Chart position. UK: 1.
'No Reply', 'I'm A Loser', 'Rock And Roll Music', 'Eight Days A Week'

'Ticket To Ride' b/w **'Yes It Is'** (Single)
UK: 9 April 1965. US: 19 April 1965.
Chart positions. UK: 1. US: 1
On the face of it, 1965 for The Beatles was simply a repeat of 1964: single, film with album and title-track single, US tour, single, album. But just as *Help!*, the film, is in dayglo sixties colour, so The Beatles music would burst into life across the year, with two of their finest albums and three top-notch singles. These add up to 30 of their greatest original songs, plus two cover versions.

If they had split up at the end of 1964, they'd still be remembered as great pop artists of the first half of the decade. After 1965-1966, their legend was secured as the *greatest* pop artists of all time.

'Ticket To Ride' (Lennon/McCartney)
Recorded 15 February 1965. John Lennon – double-tracked lead vocals, rhythm guitar; Paul McCartney – backing vocals, bass, lead guitar; George Harrison – rhythm guitar, 12 string electric; Ringo Starr – drums, tambourine, handclaps.

As The Beatles move into their middle period, they make it sound so easy.

'Ticket To Ride' was recorded at the band's first session for almost four months. Across six productive days they recorded both sides of their new single, several songs for their next album and two unused outtakes just ahead of flying to the Bahamas to start their second film.

15 February 1965: 'Ticket To Ride', 'Another Girl', 'I Need You'
16 February 1965: 'I Need You', 'Another Girl', 'Yes It Is'
17 February 1965: 'The Night Before', 'You Like Me Too Much'
18 February 1965: 'You've Got To Hide Your Love Away', 'If You've Got Trouble', 'Tell Me What You See'
19 February 1965: 'You're Going To Lose That Girl'
20 February 1965: 'That Means A Lot'

'Ticket To Ride' introduced some novel musical ideas.

Firstly, Ringo's off-kilter drum pattern, which was suggested by Paul, probably gave rise to John's claim that 'Ticket To Ride' was the first heavy metal song.

'I liked it, 'cause it was slightly a new sound at the time,' he told David Sheff in 1980. 'It's pretty fuckin' heavy for then. If you go and look in the charts for what other music people were making, and you hear it now, it doesn't sound too bad. It's a heavy record, and the drums are heavy, too. That's why I like it.'

Whilst we should take many of John's utterances with large doses of salt, if you change the sounds of the drums and distort the guitars then you can see his point: it's easy to imagine Queens Of The Stone Age playing 'Ticket To Ride'. It's certainly heavier than anything else in the charts in April 1965. Versions by Vanilla Fudge (1967) and The Carpenters (1969) bear this out. We're just kidding about The Carpenters, but we love their version too.

The band sticks to a single chord for the first twenty seconds. The drone-like tonality is a precursor to their fascination with Indian music. They hold back in their performance, leaning back into the beat and resisting any temptation to push, or rush, until the final seconds when they go nuts, with Paul's squalling guitar leading the way. John also channels Bob Dylan in the 'ah' at 1.41.

'Ticket To Ride' was The Beatles' seventh consecutive number-one hit in the United Kingdom and their eighth overall in the US. Check out the awesome, joyful live performance at the *NME* poll-winners' concert in Wembley on 11 April 1965.

'Yes It Is' (Lennon/McCartney)

Recorded 16 February 1965. John Lennon – double-tracked lead vocals, classical guitar; Paul McCartney – backing vocals, bass; George Harrison – backing vocals, lead guitar; Ringo Starr – drums, tambourine.

'Yes It Is', for all its merits, is an obvious development of 'This Boy', sharing that song's 12/8 time signature, sophisticated three-part vocal harmonies and some of its doo-wop chord changes. It does have more musical ideas, with some glorious chords and full-throated vocals in the bridge section, which ends with a sighing 'yes it is, yeah'.

'John is nothing if not consistent in the style of his wordplay,' suggests Alan W Pollack. 'The red/blue pun which runs through the current song has as its precedents not only the black/blue obvious example of 'Baby's In Black', but also the this/that motif of 'This Boy', and many others as well. A number of equally familiar verbal pirouettes reappear here, some of which go beyond cleverness to hint at emotional content with almost subconscious indirection. We have, for example: a vague reference to something spoken offline from the song proper ('remember what I said tonight'), a hint that the hurt of love lost is exacerbated by a feeling of public humiliation ('everybody knows, I'm sure'; and 'but it's my pride'), and just plain small talk clichés thrown in for good measure (the title phrase, and 'it's true.')'

Nevertheless, although it doesn't fit with the rest of the *Help!* album, it's a worthy song from when B-sides were worth flipping your 7' single to hear.

Beatles For Sale No. 2 EP (UK)

4 June 1965.
Chart position. UK: 2.
'I'll Follow The Sun', 'Baby's In Black', 'Words Of Love', 'I Don't Want To Spoil The Party'

Beatles VI (US album)

14 June 1965.
Chart position. US: 1.
'Kansas City', 'Hey, Hey, Hey, Hey', 'Eight Days A Week', 'You Like Me Too Much', 'Bad Boy', 'I Don't Want To Spoil The Party', 'Words Of Love', 'What You're Doing', 'Yes It Is', 'Dizzy Miss Lizzy', 'Tell Me What You See', 'Every Little Thing'

Beatles VI gathers the remaining songs from *Beatles For Sale* absent from *Beatles '65* including the US-only number one single 'Eight Days A Week'. To this, it adds a fabulous B-side ('Yes It Is'), two cover versions that were recorded specifically for the US market ('Bad Boy' and 'Dizzy Miss Lizzy') and two new recordings which would not be released in the UK for another two months ('Tell Me What You See' and 'You Like Me Too Much').

As with *The Beatles Second Album*, this is a strong collection of songs which hold together remarkably well. It was the band's fifth number one in the US.

'Bad Boy' (Williams)

Recorded 10 May 1965. John Lennon – vocals, rhythm guitar; Paul McCartney – bass, electric piano; George Harrison – lead guitar; Ringo Starr – drums, tambourine.

'Bad Boy' had been in the band's set between 1960 and 1962. For this studio version they quickly recorded four takes of the backing track then overdubbed lead vocals (John), second lead guitar which closely matches the original (George), electric piano (Paul) and tambourine (Ringo). Their version of Williams' 'Dizzy Miss Lizzy' dates to this same session.

It would be another eighteen months until 'Bad Boy' snuck out on a greatest hits' compilation in the UK.

'Help!' b/w **'I'm Down'** (Single)

UK: 23 July 1965. US: 19 July 1965.
Chart positions. UK: 1. US: 1.

The band's tenth single for EMI, an energetic and catchy A-side, and a fun, rocking B-side.

'Help!' (Lennon/McCartney)

Recorded 13 April 1965 (stereo version); 13 April and 24 May 1965 (mono version). John Lennon – double-tracked vocals, 12-string acoustic guitar; Paul McCartney – backing vocals, bass; George Harrison – backing vocals, lead guitar; Ringo Starr – drums, tambourine.

Paul McCartney (in *Many Years From Now* by Barry Miles): 'I seem to remember Dick Lester, Brian Epstein, Walter Shenson and ourselves sitting around… and thinking, What are we going to call this one? Somehow *Help!* came out. I didn't suggest it; John might have suggested it or Dick Lester. It was one of them. John went home and thought about it and got the basis of it, then we had a writing session on it. We sat at his house and wrote it, so he obviously didn't have that much of it. I would have to credit it to John for original inspiration 70-30. My main contribution is the countermelody to John.'

'Help!' mixes a driving beat, some direct and anxious lyrics, and a spiralling lead guitar line with the folky feel of a 12-string guitar. In thematic terms, this sits with 'You Can't Do That', 'I'll Cry Instead', 'Tell Me Why', 'I'm A Loser' and 'I Don't Want To Spoil The Party' as the last series of songs in 1964-1965 that unusually cover topics of resentment and misery.

A full set of takes available in collectors' circles shows the band working through the arrangement of the backing track in EMI's Studio 2 between 7 pm and 10 pm on 13 April 1965.

The basic track includes an acoustic 12-string rhythm guitar (John), lead guitar (George), bass (Paul) and drums (Ringo). Take 1 breaks down after twenty seconds when a string breaks on John's guitar. Take 2 gets half way through the first verse – Ringo's snare has an appealing snap to its sound. Take

3 is more complete. The band are super-tight but only manage to start verse 2 when the takes ends. George is struggling with the rapid guitar arpeggios ('they're just so fast', he explains) and he agrees with George Martin to overdub them later. Take four excludes the lead guitar and John taps the top of his acoustic guitar to keep time. They get halfway through the second verse when John loses his rhythm and the take breaks down. Take five is complete, takes six and seven ends when John needs to retune his guitar and they lose their way on take eight. Take nine is complete and is the first with an attempt to add overdubbed vocals. These were polished in subsequent overdub takes, including backing vocals that anticipate the lead vocals rather than echo them – listen to 'Shine' by Take That (a number one in the UK in 2006) for an obvious descendant of this novel idea. George's lead guitar is added at take 12.

Perhaps the most remarkable part of the song is when John's voice jumps to falsetto, first heard at 0.46. We also have a marvellous drop in dynamics in the third verse (at 1.31) as the song closes in on itself. The band re-join in turn until a thrilling Ringo snare crescendo (1.50) kicks the song back into first gear and accelerates the song to its conclusion with swing and precision.

John's 12-string Framus guitar was thought to be lost until it was discovered in the attic of rural family home just outside London, having been missing for over 50 years. It was sold for £2.3m in May 2024, the most expensive Beatles instrument ever sold at auction.

Collectors can track down several mixes. The most commonly available is a 1987 remix which is on the CD reissue and the *One* compilation album. The original 1965 stereo mix can be heard on the 2009 box set *The Beatles In Mono* (go figure). A new stereo mix was completed in 2015 for the Blu-Ray *One+*, and Giles Martin employed the MAL algorithm for another new mix released in 2023 on the re-release of *The Beatles 1962-1966*. The mono mix from 1965 has a different lead vocal than the stereo mixes and has the intro spliced on. This is most easily heard on the original single A-side or the 2009 mono-reissue of the *Help*! album.

'I'm Down' (Lennon/McCartney)

Recorded 14 June 1965. Paul McCartney – lead vocals, bass; John Lennon – backing vocals, rhythm guitar, organ; George Harrison – backing vocals, lead guitar; Ringo Starr – drums, bongos.

'I'm Down' owes a debt to Little Richard's 'Long Tall Sally' but with a deft humour typical of Paul McCartney.

> We're all alone and there's nobody else
> You still moan, 'Keep your hands to yourself!'

We also have a simply outrageous organ solo (1.19 to 1.37), after which Ringo speeds up significantly, and adds bongo fury in the last minute or so – very audible in the stereo mix.

'I'm Down' replaced 'Long Tall Sally' as the band's closing number in their live shows throughout 1965 and 1966. This includes their famous concert at Shea Stadium on 15 August 1965, giddily performing to a crowd of 55,600 – their largest ever.

'Because I did the organ on 'I'm Down', I decided to play it on stage for the first time,' John said. 'I didn't really know what to do because I felt naked without a guitar, so I was doing all Jerry Lee – I was jumping about and I only played about two bars of it.'

Footage of John playing his Vox Continental organ with his elbows is one of the highlights of the marvellous film of the Shea Stadium performance. George can hardly play for laughing.

This might be a fun, trite song, but you cannot deny that it's full of panache.

Help! (UK album)

6 August 1965.
Chart position. UK: 1.

1965 was The Beatles' annus miraculous.

The *Help!* album was, as usual, recorded under great pressure; this time either side of filming commitments. We see a clear development of the band's musical palette with electric piano, a string quartet, flutes and acoustic guitar featured. George's songwriting starts in earnest with 'You Like Me Too Much'

The sessions were recorded for better stereo mixing, with guitars placed on different tracks to bass and drums, allowing the rhythm section to be centred in the stereo image. There are two cover versions, one successful – the country bounce of 'Act Naturally'– and one that can be comfortably skipped – the tired rock and roll of 'Dizzy Miss Lizzy'.

Help! is a transitional album containing some killer songs, hints of the sophistication that will colour *Rubber Soul*, some clues about what will come in 1966 and several final nods to the past. It was nominated as Album Of The Year at the 1966 Grammys Awards. This was the first time that a rock band had been recognised in this category. To this day it still sounds fresh and enjoyable.

'Help!'

Previously released as a single.

'The Night Before' (Lennon/McCartney)

Recorded 17 February 1965. Paul McCartney – double-tracked lead vocals, bass, lead guitar; John Lennon – electric piano, backing vocals; George Harrison – rhythm guitar, lead guitar, backing vocals; Ringo Starr – drums, maracas.

Pop with a bluesy undercurrent, 'The Night Before' is led by John's groovy Hohner Pianet electric piano and Paul's marvellous singing. It's featured in the *Help!* film during a scene filmed on a breezy Salisbury Plain in early May 1965.

They pull out a large of cache of chords: the song is in D and the intro climbs through F and G7 to A7 before tumbling into first line of the verse with D, C, G and A (repeated) before a switch to Bm, Gm6, D and G7 then a quick and unexpected flip to F ('treat me like you *did*') and G. The bridge starts in Am and D7 then G, before resolving through Bm, E7 and A7. That's twelve different chords. Keeping up?

Paul's vocal lead is double-tracked throughout and he adds a sweet little twist in the final phrase of the verse: 'treat me you dee-yid'.

'You've Got To Hide Your Love Away' (Lennon/McCartney)

Recorded 18 February 1965. John Lennon – vocals, 12-string acoustic guitar; Paul McCartney – bass, maracas; George Harrison – classical guitar, 12-string acoustic guitar; Ringo Starr – brushed snare drum, tambourine; John Scott – tenor and alto flutes.

'You've Got To Hide Your Love Away' was composed with just four major chords and is mostly acoustic. A beginner can learn this mellow tune on the guitar in minutes. Even novices would appreciate that odd-sounding F chord under 'turn my face to the wall'. Here is another example of that flat-seventh seen previously in 'A Hard Day's Night' and others which marries folk to rock.

Is it about Brian Epstein? That's mere conjecture. The Bob Dylan influence is clear, to our ears, however, with its acoustic feel and introspective lyrics. Compare Lennon's first verse with Dylan's 'I Don't Believe You (She Acts Like We Never Have Met') from 1964.

Here I stand, head in hands/Turn my face to the wall
If she's gone I can't go on/Feeling two foot small

I can't understand, she let go of my hand/And left me here facing the wall
I'd sure like to know why she did go/But I can't get close to her at all

Ironically, just four weeks before The Beatles recorded 'You've Got To Hide Your Love Away', Dylan had picked up an electric guitar and recorded his first electric half-an-album, *Bringing It All Back Home*.

We should also mention flautist Johnnie Scott, who was the first of many hired session musicians who would add instrumentation to Beatles songs, which none of the band or producer George Martin could play themselves (we're not counting Andy White here, before you complain).

'I Need You' (Harrison)

Recorded 15–16 February 1965. George Harrison – double-tracked lead vocals, classical guitar, 12-string electric guitar; John Lennon – acoustic guitar, backing vocals, snare drum; Paul McCartney – backing vocals, bass; Ringo Starr – percussion, cowbell.

At last, here comes George Harrison, songwriter. Within a year, and the five songs on *Rubber Soul* and *Revolver*, George would be the equal of John and Paul. Not so long after that, his majestic *All Things Must Pass* would mark the best of all of their solo albums.

Like the earlier, less-developed 'Don't Bother Me', 'I Need You' has an air of vulnerability. For a very private man, 'I Need You' is alarmingly direct: 'Please come on back to me, I'm lonely as can be, I need you.' George plays acoustic guitar on the basic track, with Ringo tapping the back of an acoustic guitar and John (of all people) playing snare drum. Overdubs double-tracked George's lead vocals and added backing vocals, cowbell and the attractive swell of a 12-string electric guitar controlled by a volume pedal.

We direct you to Tom Petty's emotional version, which was performed at the Concert For George in 2002.

'Another Girl' (Lennon/McCartney)

Recorded 15–16 February 1965. Paul McCartney – double-tracked lead vocals, bass, lead guitar; John Lennon – backing vocals, rhythm guitar; George Harrison – backing vocals, acoustic guitar; Ringo Starr – drums.

'Another Girl' was written by Paul on holiday in early February 1965. It's not in the top half of Beatles classics, but, as always, you have to admire its craft. The off-kilter lead guitar is by Paul as well, replacing earlier work by George.

Written in Tunisia and recorded in London, in the *Help*! film, the group performed 'Another Girl' in the Bahamas. This multi-nationality overstates the importance of this minor, if pleasing, song.

'You're Going To Lose That Girl' (Lennon/McCartney)

Recorded 19 February, 30 March 1965. John Lennon – double-tracked lead vocals, rhythm guitar; Paul McCartney – backing vocals, bass, piano; George Harrison – backing vocals, lead guitar; Ringo Starr – drums, bongos.

The last of the songs recorded for the *Help!* film, 'You're Going To Lose That Girl', sees The Beatles miming in a mocked-up recording studio environment at Twickenham Studios where, only four years later, they would fall apart making *Let It Be*. It's a final return to the Motown influence of The Marvelettes and The Miracles. Later in the year, they would explore the earthier Stax soul sound of Memphis on *Rubber Soul*. John's vocals are particularly expressive: Paul and George back him up with an exhilarating call-and-response.

The recording was left incomplete due to filming commitments in The Bahamas (22 February – 10 March), Austria (13 – 20 March) and the UK (24 March – 3 April). It was finally completed on a day off, 30 March, with final overdubs of lead guitar, bongos and piano. They returned to filming on and off until the middle of May.

'Ticket To Ride'

Previously released as a single.

'Act Naturally' (Morrison/Russell)

Recorded 17 June 1965. Ringo Starr – lead vocals, drums; Paul McCartney – backing vocals, bass; John Lennon – acoustic guitar; George Harrison – lead guitar.

The Beatles returned to EMI in June 1965 for three days of sessions to record the remainder of the *Help!* album, a B-side, and an outtake that would be revisited several months later.

14 June: 'I've Just Seen A Face', 'I'm Down', 'Yesterday'
15 June: 'It's Only Love'
17 June: 'Yesterday', 'Act Naturally', 'Wait'

Of course, Ringo needed a song to sing. They had attempted a Lennon/McCartney song called 'If You've Got Trouble' on 18 February. It was so bad that they abandoned it – a very rare example of The Beatles rejecting an original song. It's on *Anthology 2* if you really need to hear it.

The replacement, a hasty cover of Buck Owens 'Act Naturally', a country-cum-rockabilly song from 1963 which was number one in *Billboard*'s Country charts in June-July 1963, sticks closely to the original and fits Ringo's style and voice like an embroidered nudie glove. George's guitar fills are perfection throughout. His low E string is de-tuned to D, and he adds a variety of sweet licks and bends. (1.07 to 1.18 as an example) which are inventive and classy and much more prominent than the Buck Owens original.

We love Ringo. Except 'Matchbox'; you can keep that.

'It's Only Love' (Lennon/McCartney)

Recorded 15 June 1965. John Lennon – double-tracked lead vocals, 12-string acoustic guitar, electric guitar; Paul McCartney – bass; George Harrison – acoustic guitar, lead guitar; Ringo Starr – drums, tambourine.

There is more sonic invention heard in the refined 'It's Only Love'. John and George use capos on their acoustic guitars and for his multiple electric guitar overdubs, he employs a heavy tremolo. John's vocals are highly tuned and taut.

The ending is particularly beautiful and part of the song that is unique to the closing seconds. For many bands, a song like 'It's Only Love' would be their crowning glory: here it's just another song tucked away on side two of a Beatles album.

It seems likely that, with only very slight changes, the first two lines of 'It's Only Love' were re-written for 'Being For The Benefit Of Mr Kite' two years later.

'You Like Me Too Much' (Harrison)

Recorded 17 February 1965. George Harrison – double-tracked vocals, lead guitar, tambourine; John Lennon – acoustic guitar, electric piano; Paul McCartney – backing vocals, bass, piano; Ringo Starr – drums; George Martin – piano.

This isn't one of George's best. Many of his songs, such as 'You Like Me Too Much', have an air of vague dissatisfaction that identifies his main songwriting trope: think of, 'Think For Yourself', 'Taxman' and 'Blue Jay Way', all grumbles to a lesser or greater degree. When the music is less inspired, as in 'Don't Bother Me' or 'Only A Northern Song', then the results are unilluminating.

'You Like Me Too Much' was recorded in the first batch of sessions and was intended for inclusion in *Help!* film. It was recorded in eight takes and uses more variety of instrumentation than any previous Beatles song. The basic take has George on acoustic guitar and vocals, John on tambourine (only in the bridge), Paul on bass, Ringo on drums, and George Martin playing Steinway piano during the intro. Overdubs added double-tracked leads vocals with Paul's backing vocals, John on Hohner electric piano (he had also played this on 'The Night Before', recorded earlier the same day), call-and-response lead guitar and jazzy piano by George and Paul respectively (1.25-1.42) and splashes of on piano from Paul during the coda (2.26-2.33).

It might be argued that these different musical textures hide an inherently weak song: overproduce the arrangement to disguise awkward transitions, for example, from the bridge to the verse at 1.03 and 1.55. Alternatively, here is the start of something – instrumentation used to add colour to specific sections of a song with no limits due to the restriction of a future intention of playing it live.

'Tell Me What You See' (Lennon/McCartney)

Recorded 18 February 1965. Paul McCartney – lead vocals, bass, electric piano; John Lennon – backing vocals, rhythm guitar, tambourine; Ringo Starr – drums, claves, maracas; George Harrison – güiro.

'Tell Me What You See' was recorded on a productive day which also saw the band start and finish 'You've Got To Hide Your Love Away' and the outtake 'If You've Got Trouble'.

It's pleasant enough, more than a mere potboiler 'work song', but with the added novelty of prominent electric piano (Paul, especially at 1.05-1.14) and some exotic percussion including claves and maracas (Ringo) and güiro (George, his only contribution, heard under the verses – a güiro is a hollow gourd with notches cut in one side, played by rubbing a stick along its surface). This adds a Latin touch heard previously in 'Ask Me Why', 'P.S. I Love You' and 'Mr Moonlight', as well as 'Besame Mucho'.

Intriguingly, some of the lyrics in 'Tell Me What You See' are strongly reminiscent of a religious motto which hung on the wall of John Lennon's childhood home

> However black the clouds may be, in time they'll pass away
> Have faith and trust and you will see God's light make bright your day

Becomes:

> Big and black the clouds may be, time will pass away
> If you put your trust in me I'll make bright your day

Wisely, considering the 'bigger than Jesus' furore of 1966, The Beatles removed the religious references for this sly borrow.

'I've Just Seen A Face' (Lennon/McCartney)
Recorded 14 June 1965. Paul McCartney – lead and backing vocals, nylon-string guitar; John Lennon – acoustic guitar; George Harrison – acoustic 12-string guitar; Ringo Starr – drums, maracas.
Paul's genius is evident in this energetic and insistent C&W-flavoured acoustic folk tune – unplugged, as it were, with no electric instruments at all.

It starts with a unique introduction (in that it's never used again elsewhere in the song) with a tempo that deceives the ear and gives a sense of acceleration into the verse. Paul's words are tightly bound, so much that you feel he'll run out of breath before the 'falling, yes I am falling' chorus.

There is a marked change in the timbre of the stereo mix at 0.55 and you can almost hear George smiling during his lovely guitar solo (1.04-1.15). Is it corny? Maybe.

'I've Just Seen a Face' was held over for four months in the US, opening the Capitol version of *Rubber Soul* in December 1965. Roger McGuinn has said that 'I've Just Seen A Face' encouraged The Byrds to introduce a country beat into their music, starting with 'Mr Spaceman' on their album *Fifth Dimension,* which was recorded in April-May 1966.

It's well-documented, but we'll say it again: Paul recorded both 'I'm Down' and 'Yesterday' on the same day as 'I've Just Seen A Face'.

Now, that's the very definition of versatility.

'Yesterday' (Lennon/McCartney)
Recorded 14 and 17 June 1965. Paul McCartney – vocals, acoustic guitar; Tony Gilbert – violin; Sidney Sax – violin; Kenneth Essex – viola; Peter Halling – cello; Francisco Gabarró – cello.
The most covered song in history, according to the *Guinness Book Of Records*, famously started in a Paul McCartney dream.

He said in *Anthology:*

> I was living in a little flat at the top of a house,' 'and I had a piano by my bed. I woke up one morning with a tune in my head and I thought, 'Hey, I don't know this tune – or do I?' It was like a jazz melody. My dad used to know a lot of old jazz tunes; I thought maybe I'd just remembered it from the past. I went to the piano and found the chords to it, made sure I remembered it and then hawked it round to all my friends, asking what it was: 'Do you know this? It's a good little tune, but I couldn't have written it because I dreamt it.'

We put forward that *Yesterday* was prompted by Henry Mancini and Johnny Mercer's 'Moon River'. Listen again to the opening line of that song from the soundtrack of *Breakfast At Tiffany's* as sung by Audrey Hepburn as Holly Golightly, specifically the drop in the opening line: 'Moon river, wider than a mile. I'm crossing you in style some*day*...'

'Some*day*', 'Yes*terday*'. Coincidence?

Both sets of lyrics have a tenderness of longing and hope, and each arrangement uses solo voice, acoustic guitar and lush strings. Furthermore, McCartney was a fan of 'Moon River'. 'It was great to meet Hank Mancini,' he said in the *Anthology*, 'because like most people, we'd loved 'Moon River'. The line 'my huckleberry friend' had done us in: after *Breakfast At Tiffany's* he was a hero.'

Other commentators have suggested Ray Charles' 'Georgia' or 'Answer Me' by Frankie Laine, which includes the lines 'You were mine yesterday, I believed that love was here to stay'.

Whatever the providence, 'Yesterday' is a mould-breaker in pop music. This exceptionally mature piece of work, which Paul had been kicking around for a few months, was a US number one for four weeks in 1966. It was voted the best song of the 20th century in a 1999 BBC Radio 2 poll of music experts and listeners and was voted the number one pop song of all time by MTV and *Rolling Stone* the following year.

It was written on piano, but when transcribed for acoustic guitar, Paul chose to de-tune his instrument by a whole tone to make it easier to play. When playing solo acoustic guitar, there's nowhere to hide: one mistake will be very obvious. Paul nailed it in two takes, but only then because he messed up the lyrics on take one (hear him smile at his error on *Anthology 2*). The string quartet – two violins, viola, and cello – was added later that same week, the day before Paul's twenty-third birthday. Let's qualify. Paul McCartney wrote 'Yesterday' at the age of twenty-two.

Producer George Martin recognised the importance of 'Yesterday' in his 1993 book *Summer Of Love*. 'The first big departure from the standard rock 'n' roll lineup occurs with 'Yesterday',' he writes, 'which was not performed by a group at all but by a string quartet accompanying a single acoustic guitar and a solo voice. Once the breakout had occurred, this process of continual experimentation and change, of musical and technical innovation, continued at top speed through *Rubber Soul* and on into *Revolver*.'

'Yesterday' is so well established in popular culture, as we write this, it's almost sixty years since it was recorded, that its shock value in 1965 has been diluted. We stand strong and declare The Beatles' 'Yesterday' as one of greatest pieces of twentieth-century art, in any medium.

It is a melody and lyric that, upon having heard it, you feel like it must always have existed.

'Yesterday' is perfect – the timing, the pitch, the performance, the arrangement, everything.

'Dizzy Miss Lizzy' (Williams)
Recorded 10 May 1965. John Lennon – vocals, rhythm guitar, organ; Paul McCartney – bass; George Harrison – double-tracked lead guitar; Ringo Starr – drums, cowbell.
From the sublime to the ridiculous? Perhaps.

'Dizzy Miss Lizzy' offers a rock and roll flourish in direct contrast to 'Yesterday'. It was recorded on the same day as 'Bad Boy' for *Beatles VI*, and is included here as an up-tempo album closer, as with 'Twist And Shout' on *Please Please Me* and 'Money (That's What I Want)' on *Beatles For Sale*.

It's professional hack work lasting a shade over three minutes.

Help! (US album)
13 August 1965.
Chart position. US: 1.
'Help!', 'The Night Before', 'From Me To You Fantasy [Instrumental]', 'You've Got To Hide Your Love Away', 'I Need You'`, 'In The Tyrol [Instrumental]', 'Another Girl', 'Another Hard Day's Night [Instrumental]', 'Ticket To Ride', 'The Bitter End/You Can't Do That [Instrumental]', 'You're Gonna Lose That Girl', 'The Chase [Instrumental]'
As with the US version of *A Hard Day's Night*, only the first eight songs from the UK album are included here, along with a series of instrumentals taken from the film soundtrack which are not by The Beatles. One of these, based on the 'James Bond Theme', precedes 'Help!' at the start of the album.

As with the band's other US albums in 1965-1966, this bastardised product destroys the impact of the overall intent.

'Yesterday' b/w **'Act Naturally'** (US single)
13 September 1965.
Chart position. US: 1.

'Roll Over Beethoven' b/w **'Misery'** (US single)
11 October 1965.
Chart positions. US: did not chart.

'Kansas City/Hey-Hey-Hey-Hey' b/w **'Boys'** (US single)
11 October 1965.
Chart positions. US: did not chart.

'Day Tripper' b/w **'We Can Work It Out'** (Single)
UK: 3 December 1965. US: 6 December 1965.
Chart positions. UK: 1. US: 1.
The Beatles' first double A-side. Both 'Day Tripper' and 'We Can Work It Out' were recorded during the sessions for their next album, the unmatchable *Rubber Soul*.

Sessions for the single and album were completed in two batches between 12 to 24 October 1965 and 3 to 11 November 1965. That's an entire album and two singles in thirteen days of sessions. These were split by the presentation of MBEs at Buckingham Palace (26 October) and two days recording a TV show in Manchester (1-2 November).

'Day Tripper' (Lennon/McCartney)

Recorded 16 October 1965. John Lennon – double-tracked lead vocals, rhythm and lead guitar; Paul McCartney – double-tracked lead vocals, bass; George Harrison – lead guitar, backing vocals; Ringo Starr – drums, tambourine.

Like 'I Feel Fine', which was recorded almost exactly one year before, 'Day Tripper' is based on a John Lennon guitar riff. Both riffs take their inspiration from Bobby Parker's 'Watch Your Step' (1961). There is also a strong influence from the soul songs released on the Stax and Motown label in 1965, especially in the syncopation of the guitars and bass (as does 'Drive My Car', recorded a few days before). Other precedents include The Temptations' 'My Girl' (1964), Marvin Gaye's 'I'll Be Doggone' (1965) and even Roy Orbison's 'Oh, Pretty Woman' (1964).

The title is a wry pun, meaning both the English seaside visitor and someone who takes recreational drugs at the weekend (a 'Sunday driver'). This first use of 'trip' in this context eluded the gate-keepers at the BBC, who would ban 'A Day In The Life' eighteen months later for 'turn you on'. It's also likely that 'she's a big teaser; she took me halfway there' disguises more earthy pursuits.

That opening riff initially follows Parker's 12-bar blues model but breaks from that pattern with F#7 and G#7 chords and despite these having no place in the blues they instinctively feel right.

The bridge section is a middle-twelve (1.21-1.41) and is almost an old-fashioned rave-up. It holds a single B chord and the voices rise to a climatic finish, which comes far too soon. But, as Alan Pollack notes, 'The prolongation of a single chord serves a very different purpose here from that of the introduction. No subtly rising expectations this time; instead, we have a powerful, total climax leading back to the final verse. Rather than continue to slavishly reflect the lyrics, the music takes us well beyond 'half way there'. Given all of this, it's fairly obvious that a second repeat of this bridge within the same song would create an absurd anti-climax.'

The switch from the bridge to the verse shows enormous control: it would be very easy to push too hard and overplay, but The Beatles always fully understood dynamics. Such dynamics are a key component of what was emerging as rock music, so here we see the band beginning to distance themselves further from their rhythm and blues roots, creating a bold, new sound with each new song.

We also direct you to Otis Redding's simply wonderful, energetic, funky cover version. For a giggle, listen to Mae West's camp take on this. It's a hoot, complete with what sounds like a striptease to Bo Diddley in the middle.

'We Can Work It Out' (Lennon/McCartney)

Recorded 20 and 29 October 1965. Paul McCartney – double-tracked lead vocals, bass; John Lennon – backing vocals, acoustic guitar, harmonium; George Harrison – tambourine; Ringo Starr – drums.

Much softer than 'Day Tripper's tough soul – Paul's yin to John's yang, if you like – 'We Can Work It Out' is mostly an optimistic Paul song. His verses are augmented by John's bridge ('life is very short') and George's idiosyncratic waltz time interlude (first heard at 0.46-0.50, and one of the first examples of a mixed metre in a Beatles song).

There is another unusual instrument that adds to the basic acoustic guitar/bass/drums backing. John plays a harmonium, a type of pump organ that is commonly used in Indian music. Here, again, is a subtle nod to the influence of music from outside the strict pop boundaries.

In 1970, Stevie Wonder covered the song on his album *Signed, Sealed & Delivered* and was released as a single (US: #13). One of your authors thoroughly dislikes this version (clue: not the one from the UK).

Rubber Soul (UK album)

3 December 1965.

Chart position. UK: 1.

According to producer George Martin*, Rubber Soul* presented 'a new, growing Beatles to the world. For the first time, we began to think of albums as art on their own, as complete entities.'

He's right. From late 1965 onwards, the rock album was moving away from a couple of singles and some rushed filler. The Beatles themselves had kickstarted this as early as *Please Please Me*,. *A Hard Day's Night* – fourteen original songs – set the standard. *Revolver*, which was significant in this respect, was just around the corner. By the end of 1966, songs with purpose and edge could be important public statements. Pop music became art. This transition started with *Rubber Soul*, one of the best albums by anyone, ever.

'Drive My Car' (Lennon/McCartney)

Recorded: 13 October 1965. Paul McCartney – lead vocals, bass, piano, slide guitar; John Lennon – lead vocals, tambourine; George Harrison – backing vocals, lead guitar; Ringo Starr – drums, cowbell.

The asymmetric opening of 'Drive My Car' is described by Alan W Pollack as, 'two measures-worth of the Beatles' most rhythmically disorienting music ever. It starts with an eighth note pickup before the downbeat but the melodic contour of the syncopated guitar part combined with the offbeat entrance of the bass guitar make it virtually impossible for you to find the meter.'

Try counting 1-2-3-4 though the introduction and seeing where you land!

According to Paul McCartney, the term 'drive my car' is a euphemism for sex. The song contains clear sexual overtones including 'You can do something in between' and 'I can show you a better time'. Paul McCartney in *Many Years From Now*:

> 'Drive my car' was an old blues euphemism for sex, so in the end all is revealed. Black humour crept in and saved the day. It wrote itself then. I find that very often, once you get the good idea, things write themselves.

The busy bass and guitar work closely together, doubling the lively two-chord riff. Paired with the punch of Paul's new Rickenbacker bass, this gives the song a powerful low-end. The arrangement was suggested by George Harrison, who had been listening to Otis Redding's 'Respect', then a minor hit. Harrison suggested that the bass and guitar parts should play similar lines in an approximation of Redding's bass-heavy sound, resulting in one of The Beatles' most effective performances of 1965. George Harrison, in *Crawdaddy*, in 1977:

> 'On 'Drive My Car' I just played the line, which is really like a lick off 'Respect', you know, the Otis Redding version – and I played that line on guitar and Paul laid that with me on bass. We laid the track down like that. We played the lead part later on top of it.'

At the end of the first verse, Paul and John sing 'I wanna be famous, a star of the screen' and George adds 'but you can do something in between'. Paul sings a G note, John sings and abrasive F and George sings C, all over an A7 chord. This creates the delightful dissonance of A7(b13)(#9) – not so far away from the sound of a car horn, we suggest. Ringo plays an unusual two-bar double-time drum phrase under this:

> Bar one – bass, snare, snare, bass, snare, snare, bass, bass
> Bar two – snare, bass, snare, snare, bass, bass, snare, rest

And if that wasn't enough, there are jazzy piano chords in the chorus (0.20-0.34) and Paul's rudimentary slide guitar solo (1.08-1.23).

This is the opening track on The Beatles' sixth album: their invention and skill shine brightly in every second. Beep-beep-yeah!

'Norwegian Wood (This Bird Has Flown)' (Lennon/McCartney)
Recorded: 21 October 1965. John Lennon – double-tracked vocals, acoustic guitar; Paul McCartney – bass, backing vocals; George Harrison – 12-string acoustic guitar, sitar; Ringo Starr – tambourine, bass drum, maracas, finger cymbals.

In some ways, the oblique, introspective, elusive and sardonic 'Norwegian Wood (This Bird Has Flown)' is a successor to 'You've Got To Hide Your Love Away'. It's acoustic, written in a similar 6/8 meter, and hints at forbidden love – although 'Norwegian Wood (This Bird Has Flown)' is much more direct in its lyrics.

Of course, the Indian influence is very clear, with George's sitar adding a distinctive and memorable motif to John's descending acoustic guitar lick. Crucially, George's playing is carefully nuanced. An earlier, fussier version, recorded on 12 October and heard on *Anthology 2*, overdoes the sitar and is much less effective.

The prominent inclusion of an Indian instrument hinted at the further development of psychedelic rock which was becoming more prominent in 1965. Certainly, 'Heart Full Of Soul' by The Yardbirds (June 1965) and 'See My Friends' by The Kinks (July 1965) hinted at what was to come by using electric rock instruments to mimic Indian textures.

The Beatles take a softer but more direct path, adding sitar to an acoustic folk song. In due course, 'Norwegian Wood (This Bird Has Flown)' can be seen as the first step in elevating Indian classical music to mainstream popularity in the West. George had met virtuoso sitarist Ravi Shankar three months before this song was recorded and they remained close friends until George's death. Other artists, such as The Byrds, The Rolling Stones ('Paint It Black') and Donovan, began integrating Indian elements into their musical approach. The pinnacle, 'Within You Without You', would best them all in 1967.

We feel that analysis of post-1965 lyrics is fraught with danger, but we will note that there are green shoots of Lennon's surreal lyrical style: 'She asked me to stay and she told me to sit anywhere/So I looked around and I noticed there wasn't a chair…'

But listen to Bob Dylan's 'Fourth Time Around' from *Blonde On Blonde,* in which Zimmy outflanks Lennon in a half-tribute/half-piss-take.

'You Won't See Me' (Lennon/McCartney)

Recorded: 11 November 1965. Paul McCartney – double-tracked lead vocals, bass, piano; John Lennon – backing vocals, tambourine; George Harrison – backing vocals, lead guitar; Ringo Starr – drums, hi-hat; Mal Evans – Hammond organ.

'You Won't See Me' was recorded in the lengthy final day of sessions for *Rubber Soul*, just three weeks before the album's release date. As with several of Paul's songs in this period it documents a crisis in his relationship with Jane Asher – see also 'We Can Work It Out' and 'I'm Looking Through You'. The lyrics are direct, almost impatient.

I have had enough, so act your age
I can't get through
You refuse to even listen

What a shame that Paul didn't write any new words for the fourth verse instead of repeating the third.

As with other tracks on this album, the soul influence is strong, especially in the immaculate backing vocals, which get more complex through each verse. Let's add Ringo's understated drumming, the playful piano, George's pre-'Taxman' guitar stabs and the bouncing bass. Listen also for the one-note Hammond organ (from 2.30) played by the band's roadie Mal Evans.

It's all perfect and another fine example of a minor Beatles song that shows impeccably high levels of craft.

'Nowhere Man' (Lennon/McCartney)

Recorded: 21–22 October 1965. John Lennon – double-tracked lead vocals, acoustic guitar, lead guitar; Paul McCartney – bass, backing vocals; George Harrison – lead guitar, backing vocals; Ringo Starr – drums.

There is some of Lennon's cod-philosophising here. Whilst the song is sung in the third person, it's clearly the latest in a long line of self-examining songs, including 'You Can't Do That', 'I'll Cry Instead', 'Tell Me Why', 'I'm A Loser', 'I Don't Want To Spoil The Party' and 'Help!'.

Sonically, it's a folk-rock song that is dominated by the singing: three-part harmony vocals from John, Paul and George. There's also a very active bass line and the bright new sound of two Fender Stratocaster guitars in the instrumental section (0.48-1.04) and coda (2.21-2.43). George would christen his Strat 'Rocky' and use it extensively in 1967-1968, including on 'Strawberry Fields Forever', 'Lucy In The Sky With Diamonds', 'I Am The Walrus' (see him playing the guitar in the *Magical Mystery Tour* film), 'All You Need Is Love', 'Hey Jude', 'Happiness Is A Warm Gun' and many others.

The band were particularly keen to ensure that the guitars shimmered, as Paul told historian Mark Lewisohn in his invaluable *The Complete Beatles Recording Sessions* (1988):

> We were always forcing [the Abbey Road staff] into things they didn't want to do. 'Nowhere Man' was one. I remember we wanted very treble-y guitars, which they are, they're among the most treble-y guitars I've ever heard on record. The engineer said, 'All right, I'll put full treble on it,' and we said, 'That's not enough', and he said, 'But that's all I've got, I've only got one pot and that's it!' And we replied, 'Well, put that through another lot of faders and put full treble up on that. And if that's not enough, we'll go through another lot of faders'... Anyway, you'd then find, 'Oh, it worked!' And they were secretly glad because they had been the engineer who'd put three times the allowed value of treble on a song. I think they were quietly proud of all those things.

No matter how many times you have listened to 'Nowhere Man', it's still as fresh and bright as sunshine. Now, let's hear a remix with the drums boosted, please.

'Think For Yourself' (Harrison)

Recorded: 8 November 1965. George Harrison – lead vocals, lead guitar; John Lennon – guitar, backing vocals, Vox Continental organ; Paul McCartney – backing vocals, bass, fuzz bass; Ringo Starr – drums, tambourine, maracas.

Dominic Pedler:

> George Harrison contributed so powerfully to The Beatles' pioneering vision of challenging tonality. A perfect example is the harmonically outrageous 'Think For Yourself' – a maverick blueprint for left-field pop-rock.

Indeed, who else used the word 'opaque' in a pop song. As usual, George has a tendency to preach in his lyrics.

> And though you still can't see
> I know your mind's made up
> You're gonna cause more misery

Writes Allan Pollack:

> I wonder about the extent to which our song here supports the notion that George's oft-stated inner conflict between his own identity and that of his Beatles' persona is nowhere more apparent than in his own music of this period. Indeed, for all of the unmistakable Harrisonian fingerprints one finds imprinted all over 'Think For Yourself' (the restless and pungent harmonies in particular), the influence of Lennon and McCartney (as seen in certain clichés of the arrangement) is equally hard to miss.

Paul's counterpoint fuzz bass added as an overdub, gives the song a real edge. It sounds like Macca makes a mistake at 1.54 but improvises his way out of it and carries on anyway. There's also a barely heard four-to-the-floor organ part from John, which adds a dense foundation.

The band's vocal overdub session was, let's say, light-hearted. Around twenty minutes circulate within collectors' circles. Parts can be heard in the *Yellow Submarine* film and in Paul's *Liverpool Collage* (2000).

'The Word' (Lennon/McCartney)

Recorded: 10 November 1965. John Lennon – lead vocals, rhythm guitar; Paul McCartney –backing vocals, bass, piano; George Harrison – backing vocals, lead guitar; Ringo Starr – drums, maracas; George Martin – harmonium.

'The Word' is a stone-cold classic, one of those album tracks that proves this band's strength-in-depth: a slice of bluesy soul-funk with glorious singing and musicianship.

The verse is a basic twelve-bar. Paul's bass-playing here is simply brilliant. George Martin adds a loud harmonium (2.02-2.12) and the vocal harmonies in the final chorus are simply outrageous. Writes Dominic Pedler:

> This incredible stretch of melodic drama illustrates that The Beatles were not afraid to spice their songs with jarring dissonance that should – in theory – have been the antithesis of mainstream pop music. [It delivers] a nightmare of vocal dissonance that was as historically unprecedented then as it remains audibly compelling today.

The message is simple: all you need is one word; all you need is love.

Listen in turn to the left and right channels of the original mix to truly enjoy the busy mix and syncopated guitar and bass. Ringo includes some trademark 'backwards' drum fills at 0.28, 0.59, 1.31 and 2.02.

Finally, Paul once said of this song, 'John and I would like to do songs with just one note like 'Long Tall Sally'. We get near it in 'The Word''.

One note or one chord? They would achieve the latter, more or less, in their own 'Tomorrow Never Knows', as would George with his Indian-influenced 'Love You To', 'Within You Without You' and 'Blue Jay Way'. And as for a one-note song, we direct you to the 2013 song 'La Canzone Mononata' ('The One Note Song) by Italian loonies Elio e le Storie Tese.

'Michelle' (Lennon/McCartney)

Recorded: 3 November 1965. Paul McCartney – lead vocals and backing vocals, acoustic guitar, bass; John Lennon – backing vocals, classical guitar; George Harrison – backing vocals, acoustic guitar, lead guitar; Ringo Starr – drums.

You think the songs on *Rubber Soul* have been pretty good so far? Hold on to your hat as we close side one with the ageless 'Michelle', which started as an exercise in Chet Atkins fingerpicking.

Paul said in *Many Years From Now*:

> There is a song he did called 'Trambone' with a repetitive top line, and he played a bass line while playing a melody. This was an innovation for us; even though classical guitarists had played it, no rock 'n' roll guitarists had played it. The first person we knew to use a finger-picking style was Chet Atkins ... I never learned it. But based on Atkins' 'Trambone', I wanted to write something with a melody and a bass line in it.'

'Michelle' was an instrumental for many years until Paul wrote some lyrics and, with John, added a middle eight inspired by Nina Simone's version of 'I Put a Spell On You'. Compare 0.33-0.37 of 'Michelle' with 1.56-2.00 of Simone's scintillating track released earlier in 1965.

Dominic Pedler: "Michelle' is not quite the gentle ballad it is always assumed to be. Play that second chord as a minor 7th and, yes, one can hear the associations with languid French film music. But substitute [with] the Gretty chord, and suddenly it's Françoise Hardy-meets-Jimi Hendrix.'

And then there are the backing vocals. They are credited to John and Paul. That might be true, but to our ears, they are so precise that they sound like multiple overdubs of a single voice, a system that Freddie Mercury would use to great effect ten years later on Queen's 'Seaside Rendezvous'. It's 'a technique which blends with the backing track to the point of absorption by it' suggests musicologist Alan W Pollack.

Either way, the backing vocals are an integral and important part of the arrangement.

'What Goes On' (Lennon/McCartney/Starkey)

Recorded: 4 November 1965. Ringo Starr – vocals, drums; John Lennon – backing vocals, rhythm guitar; Paul McCartney – backing vocals, bass; George Harrison – lead guitar.

No doubt conscious of their problems writing a suitable song for Ringo on *Help!*, Lennon pulled out and polished this simple, older song, dating back to Quarry Men days, refurbished for *Rubber Soul*. Only the chorus was retained, with new verses possibly written by Paul. Ringo is given a co-writing credit for a contribution to the lyrics, probably the line, 'waiting for the tides of time'.

Ringo's sad-and-lonely spotlight track is one of his best contributions to a Beatles album. It suits him well, even if it lacks the depth evident elsewhere on the album. His shuffle is impeccable.

For an alternative view of this song, play the 1987 remix for the *Rubber Soul* CD. The bass, drums and Ringo's vocals are panned hard left, so isolate the right channel to expose Paul and John's gorgeous harmonies and George's rockabilly guitar playing, especially in his homage to Scotty Moore in his solo (1.34-1.55).

Listen closely during the verse before the lead break after Starr sings 'tell me why', Lennon says (at 1.28 in the left channel), 'We already told you why!'

'Girl' (Lennon/McCartney)

Recorded: 11 November 1965. John Lennon – lead vocals, acoustic guitar; Paul McCartney – backing vocals, bass; George Harrison – backing vocals, acoustic guitar, 12-string guitar; Ringo Starr – drums.

The last complete song recorded for *Rubber Soul*, the restless 'Girl' is a folk ballad which mixes acoustic guitar, a two-step oom-pah rhythm, a Greek-sounding 12-string (1.31-1.50 and more prominently from 2.01 to 2.20) and a textbook, intensely delivered lead vocal from John Lennon.

That vocal begins immediately, with no pre-amble, viz: 'She Loves You', 'It Won't Be Long', 'All My Loving', 'Can't Buy Me Love', 'You're Going To Lose That Girl' and 'Wait'. The later 'Happiness Is A Warm Gun' uses the same trick.

We particularly like the swooning drop to 'ah girl' in the chorus and the crescendo in the middle eight from 1.00 to 1.20.

Rumours that the band sing 'tit, tit, tit, tit' in the backing vocals are true. Paul said in *Many Years From Now:*

> It was amusing to see if we could get a naughty word on the record. The Beach Boys had a song out where they'd done 'la la la la' and we loved the

> innocence of that and wanted to copy it but not use the same phrase. So we were looking around for another phrase – 'dit dit dit dit,' which we decided to change it in our waggishness to 'tit tit tit tit.' And it gave us a laugh. It was good to get some light relief in the middle of this real big career that we were forging. If we could put in something that was a little bit subversive, then we would. George Martin would say, 'Was that 'dit-dit' or 'tit-tit' you were singing?' 'Oh! 'dit-dit' George, but it does sound a bit like that, doesn't it?' Then we'd get in the car and break down laughing.

John's intake of breath (first heard at 0.24) can be interpreted in several ways. If you're English, it's the sound of disbelief. If you're Italian, it's a masculine response to a good-looking woman. If you smoke pot, it's an unsubtle reference to drawing on a reefer. We suggest that you decide for yourself.

'I'm Looking Through You' (Lennon/McCartney)

Recorded: 10–11 November 1965. Paul McCartney – double-tracked vocals, bass; John Lennon – backing vocals, acoustic guitar; George Harrison – lead guitar, tambourine; Ringo Starr – drums, matchbox, Hammond organ.

Paul McCartney is a force of nature on the quietly rocking 'I'm Looking Through You'. Just the last nine seconds are blissful. It's another song about Jane Asher… see also 'You Won't See Me' and 'We Can Work It Out.

The lines 'you don't look different, but you have changed' and 'love has a nasty habit of disappearing overnight' are sung so lightly but cut deep: simple but devastating.

The Beatles were determined to get this song right. An earlier take from 24 October is missing the 'why, tell me why' middle eight and can be heard on *Anthology 2*. A remake from 6 November was also binned. The North American stereo version of *Rubber Soul* contains two false guitar starts which were cut from the other mixes.

Ringo plays the organ stabs at 0.28 and elsewhere. George's guitar doesn't enter until 0.49 and adds colour at key moments. Paul goes nuts from 2.09 with a wonderful extemporisation which foretells 'Got To Get You Into My Life' and others to come.

'In My Life' (Lennon/McCartney)

Recorded: 18 & 22 October 1965. John Lennon – double-tracked vocals, rhythm guitar; Paul McCartney – backing vocals, bass; George Harrison – backing vocals, lead guitar; Ringo Starr – drums, bells; George Martin – piano, tambourine.

'In My Life' is a candidate for John Lennon's best-ever song. He described it as his 'first real major piece of work' in a 1980 interview.

Other than the piano solo, this track uses the classic two-guitar/bass/drums instrumentation. It sounds so easy, but authorship is disputed. The lyrics are Lennon's, reworked from an earlier draft. Paul has claimed that he wrote all of the music, whereas Lennon claims that it's his, other than the middle eight.

Musicologists have used AI to analyse the song in an attempt to settle the argument. We suggest that you simply sit back and enjoy this masterpiece.

What sounds like a harpsichord solo in the middle (1.29 to 1.46) is a clever studio trick by George Martin.

Martin, in *Anthology*:

> 'In My Life' is one of my favourite songs because it is so much John. A super track and such a simple song. There's a bit where John couldn't decide what to do in the middle and, while they were having their tea break, I put down a baroque piano solo, which John didn't hear until he came back. What I wanted was too intricate for me to do live, so I did it with a half-speed piano, then sped it up, and he liked it.

The process of slowing down the backing track allowed Martin to play the solo at half the speed and one octave below the finished solo. It sounds 'right' and is an effect that, even now, would be impossible to replicate with such clarity and precision, even with pro-tools.

'In My Life' is 2.27 of sheer brilliance: if anyone ever suggests that The Beatles were 'over-rated', and some do, play them this song.

As for George Martin, his cover version from his album *In My Life* features lead vocals by Sean Connery. We've listened to this, so you don't have to.

'Wait' (Lennon/McCartney)

Recorded: 17 June and 11 November 1965. John Lennon – double tracked vocals, rhythm guitar; Paul McCartney – double tracked vocals, bass; George Harrison – lead guitar; Ringo Starr – drums, maracas, tambourine.

'Wait' is a discarded song from the *Help!* sessions, dusted off and spruced up with extra percussion in a last-session, late addition to *Rubber Soul*.

It has a stop/start arrangement, with John taking lead vocal in the verses (with harmonies) and Paul singing the middle eight, then the full band kicking in on 'Wait! Till I come back to your side, we'll forget the tears we've cried...'

We have a reminder of George's volume-swell guitar used on 'Yes It Is' and 'I Need You' and an emphatic slowing-down in the final seconds as the Beatles rattle their percussion.

This might be a minor song on a major album, but it's classy nevertheless.

'If I Needed Someone' (Harrison)

Recorded: 16 and 18 October 1965. George Harrison – double-tracked lead vocals, lead guitar; John Lennon – backing vocals, rhythm guitar; Paul McCartney – backing vocals, bass; Ringo Starr – drums, tambourine; George Martin – harmonium.

George Harrison's 'If I Needed Someone' nicks the guitar riff and melody from The Byrds' 'The Bells Of Rhymney', a Pete Seeger song about a Welsh mining disaster, released in August 1965, some four months before *Rubber*

Soul. The rhythm part sounds an awful lot like 'She Don't Care About Time', the B-side of 'Turn! Turn! Turn!' released two weeks before the recording session for 'If I Needed Someone', and we could argue that the step-wise introduction of instruments and vocals calls back to 'Day Tripper', not coincidentally recorded earlier the same day.

Dominated by a 12-string electric guitar (played with a capo at the seventh fret), there are several hints and nods to George's interest in Indian music in the harmonic choices and one-note drone effect. The lyrics, too, are unusual. They are obstinate and ambivalent, just as John and Paul's backing vocals are glorious. In particular, John's vocals bring a cutting edge on top of George's plaintive singing.

This was the only Harrison-composed song that The Beatles performed in concert. From December 1965 through August 1966, this was George's vocal spotlight as the third song of the set. Eight live recordings from 1966 survive. Fellow EMI artists The Hollies recorded a cover of 'If I Needed Someone' in advance of the release of *Rubber Soul*. It was issued on the same day and dropped into the UK top 20: George's first hit single as a composer.

'Run For Your Life' (Lennon/McCartney)

Recorded: 12 October 1965. John Lennon – vocals, acoustic 12-string guitar, slide guitar; Paul McCartney – backing vocals, bass; George Harrison – backing vocals, rhythm guitar, lead guitar; Ringo Starr – drums, tambourine.

The first song recorded for *Rubber Soul* is also its least successful. The lyric is trite, crass and definitely in bad taste. We'll simply record that John Lennon later said that he regretted the way he treated women when he was younger.

The guitar solo (0.59-1.13) is surely Lennon's work. George is brilliant, though, with many characteristic classy little fills. Let's leave it there, shall we?

Rubber Soul (US album)

6 December 1965.

Chart position. US: 1.

'I've Just Seen A Face', 'Norwegian Wood (This Bird Has Flown)', 'You Won't See Me', 'Think For Yourself', 'The Word', 'Michelle', 'It's Only Love', 'Girl', 'I'm Looking Through You', 'In My Life', 'Wait', 'Run For Your Life'

American listeners were given a wholly different version of *Rubber Soul*. Four songs were held back ('Drive My Car', 'Nowhere Man', 'If I Needed Someone' and 'What Goes On'), and two leftovers from the US *Help!* were added ('I've Just Seen A Face' and 'It's Only Love'). The result was a hugely popular and influential album in the US, but American listeners were surely short-changed.

Opening with the acoustic 'I've Just Seen A Face' rather than the soulful 'Drive My Car' and adding the quieter, more reflective 'It's Only Love' gives the American *Rubber Soul* a folkier feeling. And while it arguably works as a full-on folk-rock album, it loses some of its magic. Likewise, The Beatles' remarkable progress through 1965 and into 1966 is more difficult to track because of the omissions on this flawed version of one of their best musical statements.

The Beatles' Million Sellers EP (UK)
6 December 1965.
Chart position. US: 1.
'She Loves You', 'I Want To Hold Your Hand', 'Can't Buy Me Love', 'I Feel Fine'

1966

'Nowhere Man' b/w **'What Goes On?'** (US single)
21 February 1966.
Chart position 3.

Yesterday EP (UK)
4 March 1966.
Chart position 1.
'Yesterday', 'Act Naturally', 'You Like Me Too Much', 'It's Only Love'

'Paperback Writer' b/w **'Rain'** (Single)
UK: 10 June 1966. US: 30 May 1966.
Chart positions. UK:1. US: 1.

Rubber Soul and 'We Can Work It Out' b/w 'Day Tripper' were released on 3 December 1965, the same day as the first concert on their final UK tour. They would perform eighteen shows in eight cities across just nine days. Apart from a one-off performance in London on 1 May 1966, it would be six months before their next (and last) tour.

With no film project settled for 1966, The Beatles had the next several weeks to themselves. They reconvened at EMI Studios on 6 April to start work on their next album and single spending most of April and May recording *Revolver*, the album that many regard as their finest. Even if you think that it's not their best, there's no denying that it heralded the advent of the album as the central element of rock music, both commercially and creatively.

The recording of *Revolver* took roughly three times longer than *Rubber Soul* – an astronomical amount for 1966.

As was their wont by now, the accompanying singles were recorded at the same sessions, too. The dates of recording and mixing are:

6 April 1966: Recording 'Tomorrow Never Knows'
7 April 1966: Recording 'Tomorrow Never Knows', 'Got To Get You Into My Life'
8 April 1966: Recording 'Got To Get You Into My Life'
11 April 1966: Recording 'Got To Get You Into My Life', 'Love You To'
13 April 1966: Recording and mixing 'Love You To'. Recording 'Paperback Writer'
14 April 1966: Recording and mixing 'Paperback Writer'. Recording 'Rain'
16 April 1966: Recording and mixing 'Rain'
17 April 1966: Recording 'Doctor Robert'
19 April 1966: Recording and mixing 'Doctor Robert'
20 April 1966: Recording 'And Your Bird Can Sing'
21 April 1966: Recording 'Taxman'
22 April 1966: Recording 'Tomorrow Never Knows', 'Taxman'
25 April 1966: Mixing 'Got To Get You Into My Life', 'Love You To'
26 April 1966: Recording 'And Your Bird Can Sing'

27 April 1966: Mixing 'Tomorrow Never Knows', 'And Your Bird Can Sing', 'Taxman'. Recording 'I'm Only Sleeping'
28 April 1966: Recording 'Eleanor Rigby'
29 April 1966: Recording 'I'm Only Sleeping', Recording and mixing 'Eleanor Rigby'
5 May 1966: Recording 'I'm Only Sleeping'
6 May 1966: Recording and mixing 'I'm Only Sleeping'
9 May 1966: Recording 'For No One'
12 May 1966: Mixing 'Doctor Robert', 'And Your Bird Can Sing', 'I'm Only Sleeping'
16 May 1966: Mixing 'Love You To'. Recording and mixing 'Taxman'. Recording 'For No One'
18 May 1966: Recording and mixing 'Got To Get You Into My Life'
19 May 1966: Recording 'For No One'
20 May 1966: Mixing 'Doctor Robert', 'And Your Bird Can Sing', 'I'm Only Sleeping'
26 May 1966: Recording 'Yellow Submarine'
1 June 1966: Recording 'Yellow Submarine'
2 June 1966: Mixing 'Yellow Submarine'. Recording 'I Want To Tell You'
3 June 1966: Mixing 'And Your Bird Can Sing', 'Yellow Submarine', Recording and mixing 'I Want To Tell You'
6 June 1966: Recording and mixing 'Eleanor Rigby', Mixing 'Tomorrow Never Knows', 'For No One', 'I Want To Tell You', 'I'm Only Sleeping'
8 June 1966: Recording 'Good Day Sunshine'
9 June 1966: Recording and mixing 'Good Day Sunshine'
14 June 1966: Recording 'Here, There And Everywhere'
16 June 1966: Recording 'Here, There And Everywhere'
17 June 1966: Recording and mixing 'Got To Get You Into My Life', 'Here, There And Everywhere'
20 June 1966: Mixing 'Got To Get You Into My Life'
21 June 1966: Recording 'She Said She Said'. Mixing 'Love You To', 'Doctor Robert', 'Taxman', 'For No One', 'I Want To Tell You', 'Here, There And Everywhere'
22 June 1966: Mixing 'Tomorrow Never Knows', 'Got To Get You Into My Life', 'Eleanor Rigby', 'Yellow Submarine', 'Good Day Sunshine', 'She Said She Said'

With the album and single finished, The Beatles flew to Germany for two shows at the Circus-Krone-Bau in Munich. These were followed by bookings in Essen and Hamburg – six shows in three days. By the end of June, they were in Tokyo for five concerts at the Nippon Budokan. Films of the Munich and Tokyo concerts prove, without any doubt, that The Beatles were no longer interested in live performances. If that decision hadn't been arrived at when they commenced the sessions for *Revolver* and 'Paperback Writer', by the time they had delivered their new songs on 22 June, then surely it was inevitable. The band's experiences in Manila in early July and two fraught weeks in the US and Canada in August would confirm their withdrawal from concerts for the foreseeable future. In the end, 29 August 1966 witnessed The Beatles' final ticketed live show.

'Paperback Writer' (Lennon/McCartney)

Recorded 13–14 April 1966. Paul McCartney – lead vocals, lead guitar, bass; John Lennon – backing vocals, tambourine; George Harrison – backing vocals, lead and rhythm guitars; Ringo Starr – drums.

Paul McCartney is chiefly responsible for this gutsy, hard-rocking, often overlooked song with an unusual lyrical subject matter – his first character study in a song. It is based on a powerful McCartney guitar riff – outtakes confirm that Paul plays this on the track – and a long verse almost entirely based on one chord, G7, with a single lift to C under 'paperback *writer*'. The entire song uses just those two chords.

The basic take was just guitar and drums, with everything else added later. Musical interest is maintained by the spiralling harmony vocals (using the canon format of overlapping phrases and sounding a lot like The Beach Boys) and, in particular, the astounding, punchy bass sound. Geoff Emerick had been promoted to the role of recording engineer and later told historian Mark Lewisohn: ''Paperback Writer' was the first time the bass sound had been heard in all its excitement. Paul played a different bass, a Rickenbacker. Then we boosted it further by using a loudspeaker as a microphone. We positioned it directly in front of the bass speaker and the moving diaphragm of the second speaker made the electric current.'

That technique, invented on the hoof and in contravention of EMI policy at the time, is now a common method for recording low frequencies, such as the kick drum. Emerick also close-miked each of the drums rather than having a single overhead microphone and added extra punch by using an electronic filter to compress the sound.

The bass guitar was recorded separately, which gave Paul a chance to spend more time working out a complex arrangement to suit the song. Paul was a master at not only composing perfect bass lines that would not only be 'in the pocket' but would leave space for the vocals or a guitar solo. Geoff Emerick's skill as an engineer would be a crucial and fundamental element of The Beatles' late-middle and mature periods.

You can have fun noting the many differences between the mono mix from 14 April 1966 and the stereo mix made six months later for *A Collection Of Beatles Oldies* (and available on *Past Masters*). In particular, in mono, Paul's guitar riff is much livelier; the delay on the vocal rounds is very different, occurring earlier, and the song lasts about eight seconds longer. The more recent stereo remixes for *1+* (2015) and the *Revolver* deluxe reissue (2022) are very good. This latter mix is most easily available on the latest version of

The Beatles 1962-1966 (2023), but, of course, we recommend the original mono over all of these.

Surprisingly, Kenny Rogers would record a sterling cover of 'Paperback Writer'. Check out the B-52s, as well. And we'll try to pretend that the similarity with The Monkees' 'Last Train To Clarksville', recorded seven weeks after the release of 'Paperback Writer' is pure coincidence.

'Rain' (Lennon/McCartney)

Recorded 14 & 16 April 1966. John Lennon – lead and backing vocals, rhythm guitar; Paul McCartney – backing vocals, bass; George Harrison – backing vocals, lead guitar; Ringo Starr – drums, tambourine.

> To describe 'Rain'… as something of a dry run for the greater degree of experimentation found on *Revolver* risks underestimating the significance of a song that gave birth to British psychedelic rock.
> Simon Philo, *British Invasion: The Crosscurrents Of Musical Influence* (2014)

> Though no sitars or other ethnic 'world music' instruments are used here, the style of the song very much connotes the style of classical Indian music by virtue of the droning harmony and the, at times, florid tune.
> Alan W Pollock *Notes On 'Rain'* (1993)

And here, tucked away on a B-side, is one of the most important songs of the 1960s.

As Simon Philo correctly observes, 'Rain' heralded British psychedelia and, with its droning guitars and odd tonal quality (achieved by slowing down the backing track), it still sounds fresh, vibrant and wholly original.

Author Robert Rodriguez notes in his book *Revolver: How the Beatles Re-Imagined Rock 'n' Roll* (2012).

> Another John song that emerged during the sessions offered some perspective gleaned from acid: that the material world we live in is merely an illusion – 'just a state of mind'. John's 'Rain' – containing more input from Paul than is commonly supposed – used the mundane topic of the weather as a vehicle to express the view (embraced by regular users of acid) that external appearances, and the sway that they have over people's moods, are irrelevant. What really matters is the meaning of within – as John would expound upon in another song ['Tomorrow Never Knows']. Given its allegorical lyrics, manipulated sounds, and droning, trancelike vibe, 'Rain' can rightly be regarded as the group's first explicitly psychedelic song. While that subtext would define the greater part of George Harrison's work well into his solo years, it was already a familiar one with John. As far back as 'There's A Place', he sang about the escape

to be found internally: 'In my mind, there's no sorrow'. But with 'Rain', he not only underscored the point by using meteorological conditions as his metaphor; he also made the very conscious decision to express his willingness to share what he knew with those who hadn't yet travelled down the same mind-expanding path.

His lesson from the acid experience was that the way to escape the weight of materialistic thinking was to recognize it as the illusion that it was. For those willing to follow, he would lead the way: 'I can show you' – 'Can you hear me?' (This implicitly Messianic message echoed the one present in 'The Word', released a few months before: 'I'm here to show everybody the light').

Ringo's sharp, anticipatory rat-tat-tat snare drum opens a dense musical backing, thickened by slowing down the recording. The original take, heard in the *Revolver* box set in its untouched basic take, sounds ridiculously fast.

Listen closely at 0.40-044. Does Paul mess up his bass part and improvise his way out?

And then, at 2.22-2.30, a highly syncopated drums and bass pattern includes a whole second of silence. This takes full advantage of Paul adding his bass after the basic take had been laid down.

'Nowhere was the benefit of this heard to greater effect', writes Robert Rodriguez, 'than at the break beginning just before the coda at 2:22. Knowing in advance what Ringo was going to play allowed for Paul to lock onto the percussive fills with precision, heightening the moment's taut drama.'

The backwards vocal towards the end (2.36-2.54) was another aural innovation and, apparently, accidental. In a 1980 interview with David Scheff for *Playboy*, Lennon recalled:

> I got home from the studio and I was stoned out of my mind on marijuana and, as I usually do, I listened to what I'd recorded that day. Somehow, I got it on backwards, and I sat there, transfixed, with the earphones on, with a big hash joint. I ran in the next day and said, 'I know what to do with it, I know ... Listen to this!' So I made them all play it backwards. The fade is me actually singing backwards with the guitars going backwards. Sharethsmnowthsmeaness ... That one was the gift of God, of Jah, actually, the god of marijuana, right? So Jah gave me that one.

Oh, and there's an *outstanding* performance by the peerless McCartney-Starr rhythm section. If anyone is ever foolish enough to suggest that Ringo wasn't world-class (or tries that old chestnut, 'not even the best drummer in The Beatles'), then play them this.

As Starr himself told *Rolling Stone* in 1984, 'I think it's the best out of all the records I've ever made. 'Rain' blows me away … I know me, and I know my playing … and then there's 'Rain'.'

'Yesterday' ... And Today (US album)
15 June 1966.
Chart position. US: 1.
'Drive My Car', 'I'm Only Sleeping', 'Nowhere Man', 'Doctor Robert', 'Yesterday', 'Act Naturally', 'And Your Bird Can Sing', 'If I Needed Someone', 'We Can Work It Out', 'What Goes On', 'Day Tripper'
This US-only album takes tracks from three different sources: the UK versions of *Help!* and *Rubber Soul* and both sides of a recent single. Despite this, and surely because of the very high quality of the band's output in 1965, this hybrid album flows wonderfully.

It was their twelfth US album and is infamous for its original cover image, known as the 'butcher cover'. This shows John, Paul, George and Ringo dressed in white coats and covered with dismembered baby dolls and hunks of raw meat. It can perhaps be interpreted it as a protest against Capitol's policy of 'butchering' their albums for the North American market. The album was withdrawn from stores and re-issued with a less controversial sleeve. Original copies are much-prized amongst collectors: a promotional mono copy was sold in 2022 for $21,000.

Nowhere Man (US single)
8 July 1966.
Chart position. US: 4.
'Nowhere Man', 'Drive My Car', 'Michelle', 'You Won't See Me'

'Eleanor Rigby' b/w **'Yellow Submarine'** (Single)
UK: 5 August 1966. US: 8 August 1966.
Chart positions. UK: 1. US: 2.

Revolver (UK album)

5 August 1966.
Chart position. UK: 1.

> There are sounds [on *Revolver]* that nobody else has done yet – I mean nobody ... ever. We'll lose some fans with it, but we'll also gain some.
> Paul McCartney, *Music And Disc Echo*, June 1966

Until recently, popular and critical opinion pointed to *Sgt. Pepper's Lonely Hearts Club Band* as The Greatest Ever. As recently as 2003, it sat atop *Rolling Stone's List Of The 500 Greatest Albums Of All Time*, with *Revolver* at #3, *Rubber Soul* at #5, *The White Album* at #10 and *Abbey Road* at #15.

In the revised 2020 list *Sgt. Pepper* has dropped to #24 behind albums by The Notorious BIG, Radiohead, Kendrick Lamar and (if you can believe it) Kanye West.

Revolver is at #11, The Beatles' second highest entry behind *Abbey Road* at #5 (behind, in order, *What's Going On*, *Pet Sounds*, *Blue* and *Songs In The Key Of Life*). Yes, there are some genuine classics on *Sgt. Pepper* – 'A Day In The Life' and 'Lucy In The Sky With Diamonds' in particular – but our view, which seems to match that of *Rolling Stone*, for what it's worth, is that *Revolver* is a more inventive, more consistent, deeper and artistically valid album than what came immediately after. Why was it not heralded as such on release? Put yourself into the mind of the average pop fan in the summer of 1966. No one was prepared for *Revolver*. It was such a huge step forward from *Rubber Soul* (an album we love), and a thousand miles from 'She Loves You', that your typical singles buyer just didn't understand it. It would be another year before the full development of 'rock' music. *Sgt. Pepper*, quite rightly, tapped into that zeitgeist and, somehow, *Revolver* was left behind.

Time and hindsight have enabled us (and *Rolling Stone*) to listen again. And the 2023 remix has made the album sound better than ever before.

So why do we think that *Revolver* is so good?

Firstly, The Beatles were maturing rapidly as songwriters in the spring of 1966. The influence of drugs on their art cannot be ignored. If *Rubber Soul* was recorded with pot, then LSD must surely be the driver of much of *Revolver*. It also marked a shift in the dominance of John Lennon and Paul McCartney: Paul was arguably the most engaged member of the band from late 1966 onwards and was very much the main driver of the *Sgt. Pepper* concept, the *Magical Mystery Tour* film, the Apple fiasco and the *Get Back* project. Without Paul, the band might well have split up in 1967 after the death of Brian Epstein.

Secondly, studio technology was now part of the creative process rather than simply a tool to capture a live performance. We have mentioned in earlier chapters where overdubs or remakes were used creatively to improve a recording. *Rubber Soul* marks the point where The Beatles considered their skills as studio craftsmen. *Revolver* allowed them to experiment. After *Revolver*, musicians creating new songs in the studio were not limited by what they could perform in concert. Only an act with the clout of The Beatles could demand the almost unlimited studio time needed to achieve this for the first time. That they were blessed with an open-minded producer, George Martin was their good fortune. And ours.

Finally, The Beatles were even more involved in the development, presentation and recording of their music. George Martin was willing to try anything, it seems. Except, in one well-documented story, agree to hang John Lennon upside down and spin him around a microphone while he sang.

Martin was joined in the control room by nineteen-year-old Geoff Emerick.

'By the time *Revolver* came along, Martin wrote almost thirty years later, 'we were into an era of trying things out like mad in the studio, an era of almost continuous technological experimentation. This went so far that on one occasion Geoff Emerick put a microphone in a bowl of water to see what it would sound like when you sang into the bowl. Needless to say, it ruined an expensive mike, and Geoff nearly got himself fired for it!'

Emerick himself recalled in his fascinating memoirs that no preparation or rehearsals took place for the songs recorded for *Revolver*. The Beatles would arrive with the outline of a song and work within the studio to achieve their artistic visions. Both Martin and Emerick were open to solving The Beatles' requests for sonic innovation, and because of this, *Revolver* expanded the studio experimentation apparent on *Rubber Soul.* Their instrumental palette was extended and new sounds included the Indian tambura and tabla, clavichord, vibraphone, French horn, saxophones, trumpets, tack piano, tape loops and sound effects. New Fender amps gave their guitars a tougher sound. The EMI engineers invented automatic double tracking (ADT), which employed two linked tape recorders to automatically create a doubled vocal track. This was used extensively in the forthcoming sessions.

With all of this open to them, *Revolver* stands firm as The Beatles' first truly artistic statement, surpassed only, we think, by *Abbey Road*.

Their most experimental work during the *Revolver* sessions was channelled into the first song they attempted, the still-remarkable 'Tomorrow Never Knows'. This set the high point for the rest of the album. From now on, anything was acceptable and anything was possible. The band's freedom of expression was very evident. They reached their mid-period apex with 'Tomorrow Never Knows', and stayed there not only for the rest of the sessions but also for three of the first four songs recorded for *Sgt. Pepper* : 'Strawberry Fields Forever', 'Penny Lane' and 'A Day In The Life', all recorded in late 1966/early 1967.

The Beatles worked hard on *Revolver*, spending as much on it, 38 days, as all of their sessions combined in 1965. The results were magical.

The album's title refers to the revolving motion of a record as it is played on a turntable. Rejected suggestions include *Bubble And Squeak*, *Abracadabra*, *Magic Circle*, *Beatles On Safari* and *Pendulum*. The striking artwork, in which ideas seem to emerge from The Beatles' head, was created by The Beatles' friend, artist Klaus Voormann, who used personal photos supplied by the band. He also subtly worked his own name and image into his drawing of George Harrison's hair. The design won Album Cover Of The Year at the 1966 Grammys.

Gramophone's jazz critic Peter Clayton observed in October 1966 that *Revolver* 'really is an astonishing collection, and listening to it you realize that the distance the four odd young men have travelled since 'Love Me Do' in 1962 is musically even greater than it is materially. It isn't easy to describe what's here since much of it involves things that are either new to pop music or which are being properly applied for the first time and which can't be helpfully compared with anything. In fact, the impression you get is not of any one sound or flavour, but simply of smoking hot newness with plenty of flaws and imperfections but fresh.'

Revolver has everything: all music is here. After sixty years, this album still sounds like the future of popular music.

And those fans that Macca feared they would lose could enjoy *The Monkees* TV show, which first aired on 12 September 1966.

'Taxman' (Harrison)

Recorded 21–22 April, 16 May and 21 June 1966. George Harrison – lead vocals, rhythm and lead guitar; John Lennon – backing vocals, rhythm guitar; Paul McCartney – backing vocals, bass, guitar solo; Ringo Starr – drums, cowbell, tambourine.

George's emergence as a gifted songwriter continues with *Revolver*'s opening track, the effervescent 'Taxman', which mixes a slab of proto-funk with a strong political statement.

Benjamin Franklin (1706-90) wrote, in 1789, 'In this world, nothing can be said to be certain, except death and taxes.'

This song mentions them both.

'Taxman' was recorded three weeks after Labour's landslide victory in the 1966 general election. Harrison learned that the band members' income tax obligations would be 95% ('1 for you, 19 for me', from the perspective of the payee).

The Beatles began recording 'Taxman' on 20 April, but the results were left unused. Starting afresh the next day, ten new takes comprised Ringo's drums, Paul's bubbling bass and George's very loud, slightly distorted and bang-on-the-nose rhythm guitar.

McCartney's bass line is not difficult to play but is very active and includes some neat melodic tricks, such as its Motown-influenced variant patterns (0.55–1.08). Paul also thickens the sound by doubling his bass line on guitar (1.32–1.44). Over the next day and a half, they added cowbell, tambourine, lead and backing vocals and an amazing rapid-fire, Indian-influenced guitar solo played by Paul McCartney (1.13-1.25).

'In those days,' George told *Guitar Player* in 1987, 'for me to be allowed to do my one song on the album, it was like, 'Great. I don't care who plays what. I was pleased to have [Paul] play that bit on 'Taxman'. If you notice, he did like a little Indian bit on it for me.'

The decision to re-use the solo at the end of the song – it's the same performance exactly, edited on – seems like a cop-out. The *Anthology* version ends cold and is more satisfying.

'Eleanor Rigby' (Lennon/McCartney)

Also released as a single.

Recorded 28–29 April & 6 June 1966. Paul McCartney – lead and backing vocals; John Lennon – backing vocals; George Harrison – backing vocals; Tony Gilbert, Sidney Sax, John Sharpe and Juergen Hess – violins; Stephen Shingles and John Underwood – violas; Derek Simpson and Norman Jones – cellos.

Whether you love or hate The Beatles you can't deny this song is pure art, which shattered the limitations of the three-minute pop single. It's a hauntingly matter-of-fact three-verse melodrama: shockingly downbeat, even morbid. The lyrics are very mature for a twenty-four-year-old: perhaps with George seeking spiritual awareness and John expanding his consciousness through lysergic acid diethylamide, then Paul, as the 'straight' one, matured quickly and worked the hardest through the rest of the band's career.

The grown-up lyrics were not your standard pop music subject matter in 1966. A detached onlooker described a lonely spinster who wears 'her face which she keeps in a jar by the door' and a secluded priest darning his socks. They are united in death as he officiates at her funeral with the vivid imagery of him 'wiping the dirt from his hands as he walks from the grave'.

For the first time, none of The Beatles play an instrument on one of their songs. Ringo Starr does not appear on it at all. The instrumentation is a classical string octet (four violinists – two of whom played on 'Yesterday', along with two violists and two cellists) performing a score composed by George Martin.

'The violin backing was Paul's idea,' John told David Scheff in 1980. 'Jane Asher had turned him on to Vivaldi, and it was very good.'

'The backing arrangement for small string ensemble,' writes Alan W Pollack, 'is well crafted by someone who clearly understood the string quartet idiom. Though eight players are used, the writing is in essentially four parts where, except for brief flashes of solo playing, each is doubled for strength.'

George Martin credits the influence of Bernard Hermann's score for the film *Fahrenheit 451*, but this is impossible as the film was not released until November 1966.

Pollack detects an affinity for the same composer's *Psycho* overture: 'Against a 'warp' of mechanical and strident chords (the effect of which is heightened by their being played in short, choppy down-bows 'near the frog' of the bow, the non-vibrato fingering, and the close miking) is woven a continuously varied and syncopated series of melodic counter-figures in either the cello or violin.'

'She Loves You' was recorded just thirty-three months before 'Eleanor Rigby'.

'I'm Only Sleeping' (Lennon/McCartney)

Recorded 27 and 29 April, 5 and 6 May 1966. John Lennon – lead and backing vocals, acoustic guitar; Paul McCartney – bass, backing vocals; George Harrison – acoustic guitar, lead guitars, backing vocals; Ringo Starr – drums.

Lennon's ode to staying in bed all day, presumably tripping on LSD, was recorded with a basic track of two acoustic guitars, bass and drums on 27 April 1966. Lennon added his lead vocals two days later. The following week, George added a backwards guitar solo (1.33-1.44). There are two solos, in fact, played simultaneously. George worked out what he wanted to play and asked George Martin to transcribe the notes so that he could play them in reverse. Listen closely for a clean guitar sound and a distorted variant. Backing vocals completed the track on 6 May.

The sluggish tempo is accentuated during the break before the second bridge. The sound of a yawn (at 1.01) is preceded by John saying, 'Yawn, Paul'.

In the US, 'I'm Only Sleeping' (along with 'And Your Bird Can Sing' and 'Doctor Robert') was released two months ahead of *Revolver* on *'Yesterday'... And Today*. The Capitol version of *Revolver* is, therefore, three songs short.

The song keeps popping up. Suggs, the singer with vintage British band Madness, took his version into the top ten in 1995. A music video, directed by Em Cooper, was released to YouTube on 1 November 2022 to coincide with the re-release of *Revolver*. It won the Grammy Award for Best Music Video at the 66th Annual Grammy Awards in 2024, fifty-eight years after the song's release.

A sequel, of sorts, 'I'm So Tired', would be recorded two years later.

'Love You To' (Harrison)

Recorded 11 and 13 April 1966. George Harrison – lead and backing vocals, lead, rhythm and acoustic guitars, sitar; Paul McCartney – backing vocals; Ringo Starr – tambourine; Anil Bhagwat – tabla; unnamed musicians from the Asian Music Circle – sitar, tambura.

We're only four songs into *Revolver,* and here we have a major new sound: the bold and striking incorporation of the Indian raga into Western pop music. The sound of sitar and tabla within a rock rhythm, and loud, distorted electric guitar deep in the mix might not have been new – both 'Heart Full Of Soul' by The Yardbirds and 'See My Friends' by The Kinks (both 1965) emulate the sound of Indian instruments and The Beatles' own 'Ticket To Ride' and 'Norwegian Wood (This Bird Has Flown)' nod to similar influences – but Indian instrumentation and structure had never been presented before in such a high-profile, explicit manner.

The composition emulates the vocal tradition of Hindustani classical music, comprising an opening *alap* (the improvised section from 0.00 to 0.35); a *gat* (the main melody from 0.35 to 2.41); and a *drut* (a fast *gat* in the final twenty seconds) to close the piece.

As with 'Taxman', 'Eleanor Rigby' and 'She Said She Said', 'Love You To' mentions death in a set of lyrics which mix philosophy with a rather detached and oblique love song.

Each day just goes so fast
I turn around, it's past
You don't get time to hang a sign on me
Love me while you can
Before I'm a dead old man

Only a year before, George was writing 'You like me too much and I like you. I really do.' The musicologist David Reck has cited 'Love You To' as being revolutionary in Western culture. 'One cannot emphasise how absolutely unprecedented this piece is in the history of popular music,' he wrote in *Asian Music*. 'For the first time an Asian music was not parodied utilising familiar stereotypes and misconceptions, but rather transferred in toto into a new environment with sympathy and rare understanding.'

Listen to the 2023 remix of 'Love You To'. This brings out the clarity of the Indian instruments, especially the tabla hand drum performed by Anil Bhagwat.

He told Mark Lewisohn:

> The session came out of the blue. A chap called Angardi called me and asked if I was free that evening to work with George. I didn't know who he meant – he didn't say it was Harrison. It was only when a Rolls Royce came to pick me up that I realised I'd be playing on a Beatles session. When I arrived at Abbey Road, there were girls everywhere with Thermos flasks, cakes, sandwiches, waiting for the Beatles to come out. George told me what he wanted and I tuned the tabla with him. He suggested I play something in the Ravi Shankar style, 16-beats, though he agreed that I should improvise. Indian music is all improvisation. I was very lucky, they put my name on the record sleeve. I'm really proud of that, they were the greatest ever and my name is on the sleeve. It was one of the most exciting times of my life.

'Within You, Without You' and 'The Inner Light' were just around the corner. These songs are the yardsticks by which the nerdiest Beatles fans can be measured. We love them, of course.

'Here, There And Everywhere' (Lennon/McCartney)

Recorded 14, 16 and 17 June 1966. Paul McCartney – double-tracked lead vocals, rhythm guitar, bass, finger-snaps; John Lennon – backing vocals, finger-snaps; George Harrison – lead guitar, backing vocals, finger-snaps; Ringo Starr – drums, finger-snaps.

'Yesterday' is rightly regarded as a cornerstone of The Beatles' back catalogue. 'Here, There And Everywhere', recorded exactly one year after Paul's most famous song, has all the beauty and melody of 'Yesterday' but with a positivity of mood that looks forward, not backwards.

'Here, There And Everywhere' is a delicate but bitter-sweet romantic ballad, exquisitely written and brilliantly performed. Paul has said many times that The Beach Boys' 'God Only Knows', one of their defining tracks, was a big influence. He told BBC Radio 1 in 2007: "God Only Knows' is one of the few songs that reduces me to tears every time I hear it. It's really just a love song, but it's brilliantly done. It shows the genius of [writer] Brian [Wilson].'

'Here, There And Everywhere' is noticeable for its poetic lyrics, whereby each word of the song's title frames each of the three verses and the layered backing vocals, which took three days to get right.

'Here, There And Everywhere' might be Paul McCartney's most perfect song. John Lennon said in his 1980 *Playboy* interview it was 'one of my favourite songs of The Beatles'. It was ranked the 4th greatest song of all time by *Mojo* in 2000, three places behind Lennon's own 'In My Life'. 'Yesterday' was eleventh.

To our ears, the final 'and hoping she's always there, I will be there' (2.00-2.06) is echoed in 'I Don't Know How To Love Him', from *Jesus Christ Superstar*: listen to 'in very many ways, he's just one more' (first heard at 1.14 on the soundtrack to the film). In passing, 'Simon Zealotes', another tune from the same Lloyd-Webber/Rice musical, sounds suspiciously like 'Lady Madonna'.

'Yellow Submarine' (Lennon/McCartney)
Also released as a single.
Recorded 26 May and 1 June 1966. Ringo Starr – lead and backing vocals, drums; John Lennon – acoustic guitar, backing vocals; Paul McCartney – bass, backing vocals; George Harrison – tambourine, backing vocals; Mal Evans – bass drum, backing vocals; Brian Jones – ocarina, backing vocals; Neil Aspinall, Alf Bicknell, Pattie Boyd, Marianne Faithfull – backing vocals; George Martin – backing vocals; Geoff Emerick – backing vocals.

'Yellow Submarine' is Ringo's first and only lead vocal on a single by The Beatles. It's a collaboration between John, who wrote the verses – there's a very downbeat early sketch on the 2022 deluxe version of *Revolver* – and Paul, who added the rousing, sing-along chorus.

It's a simple song, just five chords. It's catchy; Ringo sounds relaxed and sings brilliantly. Anyone from five to eighty years old can learn the chorus and join in.

The flippant, fun, carnival feeling and marching rhythm of 'Yellow Submarine' may have been suggested, or at least validated, by Bob Dylan's 'Rainy Day Women #12 and 35' which was lodged in the UK top ten when The Beatles added a party atmosphere to 'Yellow Submarine' on 1 June 1966. Onto a spare track on the master tape, they added, in rough order of appearance, John Lennon blowing bubbles into water using a straw, George Harrison swirling water in a metal bathtub, two ships' bells, a football rattle, party atmosphere voices, an ocarina played by The Rolling Stones' Brian Jones, coins and a foghorn. Another track contains chains being rattled in the bathtub, clinking glasses, more chatter, a brass band (sources disagree on whether musicians were booked especially for the session or whether George Martin used a library recording), John shouting naval phrases, whooshing effects and a marching band drum played by Mal Evans. The final chorus was sung by anyone in the studio, including Mal Evans, Neil Aspinall, George

Martin, Geoff Emerick, Pattie Harrison, Brian Jones, Marianne Faithfull and The Beatles' driver Alf Bicknell.

'Eleanor Rigby' b/w 'Yellow Submarine' was a UK number one for four weeks in August and September 1966. Wait ... a double A-side comprising 'Eleanor Rigby' – a pessimistic kitchen sink drama with piercing strings – and 'Yellow Submarine, a kids' song crooned by the drummer? Whichever side you played, it ain't rock and roll. But it is The Beatles.

'She Said She Said' (Lennon/McCartney)

Recorded 21 June 1966. John Lennon – lead and backing vocals, rhythm guitar, Hammond organ; Paul McCartney – bass (perhaps); George Harrison – backing vocals, bass (probably), lead guitar; Ringo Starr – drums, shaker.

If 'Not A Second Time' is an unheralded song in John Lennon's development as a songwriter, then here's another. What an outstanding track!

Originally titled 'He Said' – John's home recordings have been available for years – this enigmatic song originated in August 1965 during a six-day break from the band's US tour. Brian Epstein had rented Zsa Zsa Gabor's house in Beverly Hills for him and the band and their retinue. The Beatles found it impossible to leave and invited guests to visit. On 24 August 1965, they hosted Roger McGuinn and David Crosby (both of The Byrds) and actor Peter Fonda.

Fonda later wrote for *Rolling Stone*:

> I finally made my way past the kids and the guards. Paul and George were on the back patio, and the helicopters were patrolling overhead. They were sitting at a table under an umbrella in a rather comical attempt at privacy. Soon afterwards, we dropped acid and began tripping for what would prove to be all night and most of the next day; all of us, including the original Byrds, eventually ended up inside a huge, empty and sunken tub in the bathroom, babbling our minds away. I had the privilege of listening to the four of them sing, play around and scheme about what they would compose and achieve. They were so enthusiastic, so full of fun. John was the wittiest and most astute. I enjoyed just hearing him speak and there were no pretensions in his manner. He just sat around, laying out lines of poetry and thinking – an amazing mind. He talked a lot, yet he still seemed so private. It was a thoroughly tripped-out atmosphere because they kept finding girls hiding under tables and so forth.

Fonda mentioned his self-inflicted childhood gunshot accident when aged ten, he shot himself and nearly died.

'We didn't want to hear about that!' Lennon told David Scheff four years later. 'We were on an acid trip and the sun was shining and the girls were dancing and the whole thing was beautiful and Sixties, and this guy – who I really didn't know; he hadn't made *Easy Rider* or anything – kept coming over, wearing shades, saying, 'I know what it's like to be dead' and we kept leaving him because he was so boring! ... It was scary. You know ... when you're flying high and [whispers] 'I know what it's like to be dead, man.'

Harrison recalled in *Anthology*: 'He was showing us his bullet wound. He was very uncool.'

Lennon eventually asked Fonda to leave, but remembered the exchange when he was writing new material for *Revolver* the next spring. The opening verses reflect the anxiety and paranoia of Fonda's words in what we can only assume is a reference to an out-of-body drug trip.

She said, 'I know what it's like to be dead
I know what it is to be sad'

As The Beatles got older, they reflected on mortality, linking this back to childhood, evident in the previous year's 'In My Life', in 'Strawberry Fields Forever' and 'Penny Lane', both recorded later in 1966 and also here, in the current song. There's a palpable lift as John sings 'when I was a boy', as the song switches to a more reflective tone, and the music modulates to a different key and changes metre from 4/4 to 3/4 (on 'no, no, no') and back again (back into to the verse). Changes of metre would colour many of The Beatles' songs from now on. See: 'All You Need is Love', 'Good Morning, Good Morning', 'Good Day Sunshine', 'Blue Jay Way', 'Happiness Is A Warm Gun' and many others.

The presence of McGuinn and Crosby in this story should not be underestimated. They discussed their interest in Indian classical music with Lennon and Harrison. Crosby recommended that they investigate the recordings of Ravi Shankar. From here, it was a short step to 'Eight Miles High' (a retelling of The Byrds' first visit to the UK immediately before the Peter Fonda encounter described here) , 'Love You To' and the assimilation of Indian influences into Western music.

'She Said She Said' was the final track recorded for *Revolver* in a single nine-hour session on 21 June 1966, two days before the band began the first leg of their 1966 world tour.

Tempers were frayed and, or so it seems, Paul left the session early and didn't record the bass part for 'She Said'. He recalled in *Many Years From Now*: 'I think we had a barney or something and I said, 'Oh, fuck you!' and they said, 'Well, we'll do it.' I think George played bass.'

Robert Rodriguez, in *Revolver: How the Beatles Re-Imagined Rock 'n' Roll* (2012) makes a strong case that George plays bass on this song, concluding, 'The bass line itself doesn't particularly resemble Paul's style... inasmuch as it doesn't really draw attention to itself. It is solid and workmanlike.'

Despite its fascinating provenance, 'She Said She Said' doesn't sit in the top tier of Beatles songs. But in the running order of *Revolver*, it fits perfectly.

'Good Day Sunshine' (Lennon/McCartney)

Recorded 8–9 June 1966. Paul McCartney – lead and backing vocals, piano, handclaps; John Lennon – backing and backing vocals, rhythm guitar, handclaps; George Harrison – backing and backing vocals, bass, handclaps; Ringo Starr – drums, handclaps; George Martin – piano.

Composed by Paul McCartney on John Lennon's piano, the pulsating 'Good Day Sunshine' opens side two of *Revolver* with a simple paean to a sunny day. It contrasts markedly with the downbeat tracks of side one, three of which explicitly mention death. There are no hidden meanings here, no exotic instruments, no tape loops, no drug references.

The springboard was songs such as The Lovin' Spoonful's 'Daydream', released in February 1966 and number one in the US when 'Good Day Sunshine' was recorded, as well as possibly The Kinks' 'Sunny Afternoon' which had been released the week before the recording sessions. What is certain is that John and George attended a concert by The Lovin' Spoonful in London on 18 April 1966.

The basic take comprised Paul (piano), George (bass) and Ringo (drums). Overdubs included a second piano from Paul, percussion, vocals and a short piano solo (0.57-1.05) by George Martin. John is credited with rhythm guitar – if so, it's buried in the mix.

The song modulates towards the end, i.e., the melody lifts by one semitone (from E to F, in this case). This trick of maintaining interest is common in pop power ballads. Take four examples: 'I Will Always Love You' by Whitney Houston (at 3.10); 'It Must Have Been Love' by Roxette (at 2.59); 'Total Eclipse Of The Heart' by Bonnie Tyler (at 4.15); 'Can't Smile Without You' by Barry Manilow (at 1.33, 2.10 and 2.31).

The Beatles hardly ever modulated. Other than 'Good Day Sunshine' (at 1.57), we have a very subtle change in 'And I Love Her' (at 1.13) and several in 'Penny Lane', which modulates at 0.32 (on 'very strange') and back to the home key (on 'meanwhile back', no less) at 0.51, repeating the trick later in the song.

'And Your Bird Can Sing' (Lennon/McCartney)

Recorded 26 April 1966. John Lennon – lead vocals, rhythm guitar, handclaps; Paul McCartney – backing vocals, bass, lead guitar, handclaps; George Harrison – backing vocals, lead guitar, handclaps; Ringo Starr – drums, tambourine, handclaps.

One popular theory is that in 'And Your Bird Can Sing' John Lennon was addressing Frank Sinatra in response to an article about the American singer in the April 1966 issue of *Esquire* magazine. The article, written by Gay Talese, mentions the filming of a TV special in which Sinatra saw 'an opportunity to appeal not only to those nostalgic, but also to communicate his talent to some rock-and-rollers – in a sense, he was battling The Beatles. The press releases being prepared by [Sinatra's PR] agency stressed this, reading: 'If you happen to be tired of kid singers wearing mops of hair thick enough to hide a crate of melons... it should be refreshing, to consider the entertainment value of a video special titled *Sinatra – A Man And His Music....*"

In the article, Sinatra refers to his penis as his 'bird'. It's not difficult to imagine Lennon thinking that Sinatra, In good Northern vernacular, was a bit of a dick. The bird in 'And Your Bird Can Sing' now has a very different meaning.

When your prized possessions
Start to weigh you down
Look in my direction
I'll be 'round, I'll be 'round

'And Your Bird Can Sing' was first recorded, appropriately enough, in the style of The Byrds on 20 April. One of the highlights of *Anthology 2* includes Lennon and McCartney laughing, unable to make their way through a vocal overdub for this first version and unable to sing due to a bad case of the giggles. One wonders if they were amused at the double meaning in the third verse: 'and your bird can swing'...

A mighty version of the song was included (without the laughing overdub) on the 2022 Super Deluxe Edition of *Revolver*. Paul's bass playing is out of this world.

Take 5, recorded on 26 April, is included on the deluxe edition of *Revolver*. This is a very basic run-through, but it is starting to get closer to the finished arrangement. The final version, take 10, is a rock powerhouse with harmony lead guitars by Harrison and McCartney and two phenomenal solos by George (0.51-1.05, 1.35-1.55).

The lyrics are cryptic.

You say you've seen seven wonders
And your bird is green
But you don't see me...

Then again, 'newspaper taxis', 'yellow matter custard' and 'goo goo g'joob' were not so far away.

Listen closely for some characteristic McCartney bass flourishes under the final verse and solo (1.22-1.52).

Finally, is it too much to suggest that the twin guitar leads of 'And Your Bird Can Sing' was a major influence on The Allman Brothers Band, Lynyrd Skynyrd, Thin Lizzy and even The Eagles (the end of 'Hotel California' in particular)?

'For No One' (Lennon/McCartney)

Recorded 9, 16 and 19 May 1966. Paul McCartney – vocals, bass, piano, clavichord; Ringo Starr – drums, tambourine, maracas; Alan Civil – French horn.

'For No One' represents Paul McCartney at his very best. It was written when he was on holiday with Jane Asher in Switzerland between 6 and 20 March 1966. It's a mature composition which shares a major-minor mood with 'Here,

There And Everywhere'. The lyrics are direct, if unsettling and enigmatic, as Paul pointedly avoids saying outright what he is really thinking.

The basic track consists simply of Paul playing a Steinway grand piano and Ringo on drums. It took ten takes to get this right. That same day, 9 May 1966, Paul added clavichord, a baroque keyboard owned by George Martin, who shipped the instrument into EMI and charged five guineas for the privilege. Ringo played maracas and cymbal, and Paul's lead vocal was added a week later, along with resonant bass and tambourine.

The only other musician heard on 'For No One' is the French horn player Alan Civil. Neither John Lennon nor George Harrison takes part in 'For No One'. Civil, who is explicitly credited on the *Revolver* album, was part of the Royal Philharmonic Orchestra, the Philharmonia Orchestra and the BBC Symphony Orchestra. He would record again with The Beatles a few months later during orchestral sessions for 'A Day In The Life'. His horn part was added on 19 May. The five seconds from 1.33, with Civil's horn providing a counterpoint to Paul's voice, piano and clavichord are delicious.

Giles Martin's stereo mix from 2022 is a vast improvement on the original 1966 stereo mix, but we recommend the original mono mix which has a much warmer vocal.

'Doctor Robert' (Lennon/McCartney)

Recorded 17 and 19 April 1966. John Lennon – double-tracked lead vocals, rhythm guitar, harmonium; Paul McCartney – backing vocals, bass; George Harrison – backing vocals, double-tracked lead guitar, maracas; Ringo Starr – drums.

'Candy Man' (Donovan, October 1965), 'Mother's Little Helper' (The Rolling Stones, July 1966), 'Doctor Robert' (The Beatles, June and August 1966). Three songs about drugs, pills, suppliers and users: 'if you're down, he'll pick you up' has no hidden meaning. The identity of the protagonist has never been confirmed, despite several possible named candidates.

Musically, it's the band's classic guitar/bass/drums beat combo, but with Harrison on maracas on the basic track. Paul's harmony vocals start in the second verse (0.32), the lead guitar enters just before the bridge (0.55), with harmonium and George's vocals in the first 'well, well, well' section (from 0.59). George sparkles on guitar through the third verse, and we must praise John's golden lead singing – very clear in the 2023 remix – and Paul's soulful backing vocals ('you're a new and better man' at 1.26 will give you goosebumps).

It's not a stand-out track on *Revolver*, but a typical album track here is better than nearly everything else any other popular artist was producing in 1966.

At 2.27, it seems too short. Always leave them wanting more, perhaps? Intriguingly, Mark Lewisohn mentions that the backing track for 'Doctor Robert' was edited from its original timing of 2.56 down to a final length of 2.13. Beatles scholar John Winn suggests that the edit is at 1.34 during the middle eight (at 'everything he can'). The removed forty-three seconds is probably another verse and middle eight: this correlates exactly with the length of these sections in the released edit from 0.59 to 1.40.

'I Want To Tell You' (Harrison)

Recorded 2–3 June 1966. George Harrison – double-tracked vocals, lead guitar, handclaps; John Lennon – backing vocals, tambourine, handclaps; Paul McCartney – backing vocals, piano, bass, handclaps; Ringo Starr – drums, maracas, handclaps.

With John Lennon providing only five songs for *Revolver* (and just two on the US variant), there was room for an unprecedented third for George Harrison. Both 'Art Of Dying' and 'Isn't It A Pity' were written in 1966: George was starting to blossom as a songwriter. In the end, the angular 'I Want To Tell You' sat perfectly in the album's running order. It starts with a fade-in and for the first seven seconds, it's difficult to work out where the beat falls.

The inarticulacy of the tongue-tied lyrics is echoed in one of the most distinctive chords in the entire Beatles catalogue, first heard at 0.24-0.32 and again at 0.46–0.53.

George, interviewed by *Guitar World* in 1992:

> That's an E7th with an F on the top, played on the piano. I'm really proud of that, because I literally invented that chord. The song was about the frustration we all feel about trying to communicate certain things with just words. I realised the chords I knew at the time just didn't capture that feeling. So after I got the guitar riff, I experimented until I came up with this dissonant chord that really echoed that sense of frustration. John later borrowed it on Abbey Road. If you listen to 'I Want You (She's So Heavy)' it's right after John sings 'it's driving me mad!' To my knowledge, there's only been one other song where somebody copped that chord – 'Back On the Chain Gang' by The Pretenders.

The song fades with repeats of the guitar riff, closing the circle of the irregular opening. The music, like the lyrics, does not offer a resolution.

'Got To Get You Into My Life' (Lennon/McCartney)

Recorded 7 April, 18 May and 17 June 1966. Paul McCartney – double-tracked lead vocals, bass; John Lennon – rhythm guitar; George Harrison – lead guitar; Ringo Starr – drums, tambourine; George Martin – organ; Eddie Thornton, Ian Hamer and Les Condon – trumpets; Alan Branscombe and Peter Coe – tenor saxophones.

The Beatles had always been big fans of American soul music, especially Motown and Stax, and were keen to record in Stax's studio in Memphis. Brain Epstein travelled to Memphis to discuss this with the studio and session dates were tentatively booked for two weeks from 9 April 1966. The news was leaked to the *Memphis Press-Scimitar* on 31 March 1966.

> The most popular recording group in the world, The Beatles of England, will come to Memphis and stay about two weeks while they make some records here, it was learned today.
> Their manager, Brian Epstein, was in Memphis a few weeks ago, stayed at the Holiday Inn-Rivermont, checking out security arrangements.
> Mrs. Estelle Axton, co-owner with Jim Stewart of Stax Records of Memphis, confirmed today that The Beatles are coming. They are scheduled to arrive April 9.
> She said they had been impressed by the Stax 'sound' on records they heard of Otis Redding, Carla Thomas, Rufus Thomas, Booker T And The MGs, and other Stax artists.
> It is planned that they will cut one album and at least one single in the Stax studio at 926 E. McLemore. In charge of the sessions will be Jim Stewart, arranger Steve Cropper and Tom Dowd, of Atlantic Records.
> Mrs. Axton said where the Beatles will stay is unsettled as yet. 'They want a house, and a suitable one is hard to find. We're not used to something like this in a town this size. We think we have located the proper house. When we make final arrangements, we'll have to fence it, and of course, it will be guarded constantly.

Paul, quoted on his website in 2022: 'The only reason you want to record in those kinds of studios is because you love the records that come out of the studios. So, we loved a lot of Stax stuff, but ultimately, I'm glad we didn't record there. EMI was our home, and we didn't have to deal with anything other than making the record. If you're in a strange studio, there's things you got to deal with, as you're getting used to the new surroundings and so on. At EMI, we knew the space and the people, so it was just a case of concentrating on making the record.'

McCartney's vibrant 'Got To Get You Into My Life' pays homage to the bold, brassy sounds of Memphis and Detroit. It's derivative, yes, but reeks of authenticity, especially the horns, which blast open the song with a rousing fanfare. Paul's singing here is amongst his best and we have one of George's greatest guitar solos: just two bars long, it's four seconds of compressed energy (1.53-1.57) with nothing else needed.

The alternative 'second version' on the *Revolver* box set sits somewhere between 'Paperback Writer' and 'Getting Better' with no horns, much more guitar and a very hippy vibe. It's glorious. It's also clear that Harrison's original guitar parts formed the framework for the horn section which was used on the final mix.

Impeccably commercial, 'Got To Get You Into My Life' was bound to be a hit for someone. It was a top tenner in the UK for Cliff Bennett And The Rebel Rousers in 1966 (very good), and a top 10 American hit for Earth, Wind & Fire in 1978 (smooth and funky) taken from the soundtrack of *Sgt. Pepper's Lonely Hearts Club Band*: a film that has to be seen to be believed.

Paul recognised its value and would perform it with Wings in 1979, on his solo tours in 1989-1991 and frequently thereafter.

'Tomorrow Never Knows' (Lennon/McCartney)
Recorded 6, 7 and 22 April 1966. John Lennon – vocals, Hammond organ, Mellotron; Paul McCartney – bass; George Harrison – sitar, tambura, lead guitar; Ringo Starr – drums, tambourine; George Martin – piano.
And so we come to 'Tomorrow Never Knows', still one of the most focused, carefully orchestrated, astonishing and compelling artworks of the twentieth century. Who knows what George Martin thought when John Lennon brought this song into the studio on the first day of sessions for a new album: the phrase 'radical departure' could have been coined for this song.

With 'Tomorrow Never Knows', The Beatles' metamorphosis from the UK's hardest working live band to creatures of the recording studio had finally completed: from the piano overdubs on 'Any Time At All' and the acoustic guitar flourishes on 'I'll Be Back' to this masterpiece in twenty-four months.

'Tomorrow Never Knows' is basically a one-chord drone, with LSD-inspired lyrics which were inspired by Timothy Leary's book *The Psychedelic Experience: A Manual Based On The Tibetan Book Of The Dead,* which John had bought a few days before the first session at the Indica Gallery in London. The shop was co-owned by John Dunbar (then married to Marianne Faithfull), Peter Asher (Jane's brother), and Paul's friend Barry Miles and was located in Mason's Yard, off Duke Street, in London's St James's district, just behind Fortnum and Mason.

The book states, on page 14: 'Whenever in doubt, turn off your mind, relax, float downstream'.

Take 1 of 'Tomorrow Never Knows', then called 'Mark One', is one of the highlights of *Anthology 2*.

The final version if based on take 3. The backing track features sitars, reversed cymbals and a four-stringed Indian instrument called a tanpura. The prominent, compressed drums are played in such a consistent manner that they sound like a repeated sample. They're not.

'The basic rhythm track was made up of a very definite rock drumbeat from Ringo,' writes George Martin, 'plus the tamboura drone, with its resonating strings. We built up a 'pad' of tamboura sounds to get continuous wafting overtones of that single drone. On top of these two main elements, which are the basis of the song, we added the voice. That vocal. True to form, John wanted me to 'do something with it'. 'I want it to sound,' he said, 'as if I'm singing from the top of a hill; I want to sound like a Buddhist monk, singing from the top of a mountain. Like the Dalai Lama. Distant, but I still want to hear it.' He wanted to make real the voice he had heard inside his head when he was reading [*Tibetan Book Of The Dead*]. Well, that wasn't asking much, now was it?'

Paul's fondness for German composer Stockhausen (1928-2007, he would be featured on the *Sgt. Pepper* cover in 1967) gave rise to the suggestion of tape loops to drop into the song at specific moments. The tape loops contain:

McCartney's laughter, speeded up (from 0.07)
An orchestral chord, a Bb major from Jean Sibelius' *Symphony No. 7* (0.19)
A Mellotron on flute setting (0.22)
A Mellotron on string setting (0.38)
One or two sitars played backward and speeded up (0.56).
Paul's guitar break (1.09-1.26) is a variant of his solo from 'Taxman', recorded the day before and has, naturally, been reversed.

Here's another anomaly. Alan W Pollack points out, '[A] 'beep' tone in the midst of the first line of the verse which follows the break; reminiscent of the phone company or radio station's hourly time check. I'm fairly well convinced that this is placed here exactly at the mid-point of the track (1:28), in a Dada-esque gesture similar to Schönberg's 'Mondfleck' number from *Pierrot Lunaire*, in which he writes an atonal fugue whose second half is the exact mirror image of its first half; keep in mind, Schönberg did this in 1913!'

You need to listen very closely, but it's there.

For Beatles obsessives, the first pressing of the UK mono version of *Revolver* used an incorrect mix (known as RM11, or the 11th mono remix). The most notable differences are the absence of the final guitar phrase from the guitar solo (heard at 1.24-1.26 in the standard mix) and a longer burst of piano at the end. RM11 was re-released officially in 2022.

Ray Davies of The Kinks didn't get it. As he wrote in *Disc And Music Echo* as the album was released, 'Listen to all those crazy sounds! It'll be popular in discotheques. I can imagine they had George Martin tied to a totem pole when they did this.'

And yet, is there a more novel and influential Beatles song than 'Tomorrow Never Knows'? You decide. But whatever you think, it's a landmark in British pop culture. This song, along with 'Rain' recorded immediately afterwards, kicked the doors down. From now on, anything was possible in the recording studio: simply capturing or preparing for a live performance was no longer *de facto*.

'Tomorrow Never Knows' has inspired countless pop and dance artists, including the Chemical Brothers' chart-topping 'Setting Sun' (1996), which was a direct tribute and includes vocals by noted Beatles enthusiast Noel Gallagher. Durable cover versions of 'Tomorrow Never Knows' by 801 (1976) and Phil Collins (1981) are worth tracking down.

'Tomorrow Never Knows' completed The Beatles' metamorphosis from Fab Four to the greatest rock band of them all. It's the last song on *Revolver*. What could possibly follow that?

Revolver (US album)

8 August 1966.
Chart position. US: 1.
'Taxman', 'Eleanor Rigby', 'Love You To', 'Here, There and Everywhere', 'Yellow Submarine', 'She Said She Said', 'Good Day Sunshine', 'For No One', 'I Want to

Tell You', 'Got to Get You into My Life', 'Tomorrow Never Knows'
Three songs from early sessions for the UK version of *Revolver* had been hived off for the American-only album *'Yesterday'... And Today*. Etiquette might have dictated that 'Paperback Writer' and 'Rain' should have made up the numbers rather than releasing this bowdlerised variant, which reduces John Lennon's lead vocals contributions from five songs to just two.

After this abomination, The Beatles were determined to stop Capitol Records' mucking up their albums. They re-signed with EMI in early 1967. This increased both their royalties and their artistic control. From now on, Capitol Records could no longer change the artwork or track listing of their new albums for American release.

A Collection Of Beatles Oldies (UK album)

9 December 1966.
Chart position. UK: 7.
'She Loves You', 'From Me to You', 'We Can Work It Out', 'Help!', 'Michelle', 'Yesterday', 'I Feel Fine', 'Yellow Submarine', 'Can't Buy Me Love', 'Bad Boy', 'Day Tripper', 'A Hard Day's Night', 'Ticket to Ride', 'Paperback Writer', 'Eleanor Rigby', 'I Want to Hold Your Hand'
With no new album due for Christmas 1966, EMI pulled together this 'best of' which includes the first UK release of 'Bad Boy', as well as the album track 'Michelle' instead of either 'Love Me Do' or 'Please Please Me'.

Conclusion

It is convenient but also arbitrary to split The Beatles' career in half. It's more realistic, in truth, to divide the period covered by this book into three. Of course, things not always being quite so cut and dried, there is no clear dividing line, but here we suggest how certain key tracks – and perhaps not the ones you might imagine – point to changes in style and approach within The Beatles' music.

The impact of these songs still resonates massively.

Early: Beatlemania – 1962-1963 'Love Me Do' to 'I Want To Hold Your Hand'

Key tracks:

'I Saw Her Standing There' – 1-2-3-faw! The first track on the first album: The Beatles rework their r&b influences into this exciting and, importantly, self-written song with a tight-as-you-like performance and oodles of energy.

'There's A Place' – anxious, tense, brilliantly arranged and sung perfectly. They're already moving beyond the obvious 'boy meets girl' subject matter.

'She Loves You' – Beatlemania encapsulated in 2.21. Pop perfection, which still has the power to thrill and surprise the listener.

'Not A Second Time' – the fourteen-bar verses and a ten-bar chorus signal John Lennon's increasing disregard for musical rules.

'I Want To Hold Your Hand' – the song that broke The Beatles worldwide. It uses all of their songwriting and performance tricks, but is effortlessly commercial.

Early Middle: Global Dominance – 1964 'Can't Buy Me Love' to 'What You're Doing'

Key tracks:

'If I Fell' – John's finest song to date has gorgeous harmonies and intricate and fast-moving chord changes adding up to a beautiful song.

'And I Love Her' – not to be outdone, Paul polishes a jewel of melody, harmony, singing and performance with a simple but perfect riff from George.

'Things We Said Today' – some outrageous chord changes and a sophisticated arrangement.

'I'll Be Back' – melancholic, restless and vulnerable, with colour added by subtle overdubs: one of the first songs that could not be reproduced on stage.

'I Feel Fine' – a bluesy riff, some C & W, feedback, a million-seller. And, for the first time, the backing track was recorded first and vocals were added later.

'No Reply' – bossa nova rhythm, sixth chords and angst.

'What You're Doing' – internal rhymes, loud bass, sonic invention and angry sarcasm.

Late Middle: Towards Maturity – 1965-1966 *Help!*, *Rubber Soul*, *Revolver*

Key tracks:
'The Night Before' – underpinned by electric piano, a new sonic texture, and a large cache of chords.
'Yesterday' – Just Paul's voice, acoustic guitar and a string quartet, a mature piece of work from a 22-year-old songwriter.
'Day Tripper' – The dynamics of rock music and tight control of performance see The Beatles moving to rockier territory.
'Norwegian Wood (This Bird Has Flown)' – oblique, introspective, elusive and sardonic. With added sitar.
'In My Life' – a candidate for John Lennon's best-ever song, using studio trickery to add a piano overdub.
'Tomorrow Never Knows' – one of the most focused, carefully orchestrated, astonishing and compelling artworks of the twentieth century. This is where The Beatles eclipsed all of their peers.
'Rain' – a truly important song, 'Rain' has outstanding musicianship, backwards masking, intensity and originality.
'Eleanor Rigby' – the track that shattered the limitations of the three-minute pop single.
'Love You To' – a brave and beautiful combination of the Indian raga and Western pop music. George Harrison, take a bow.
'She Said She Said' – changes in metre anticipate the experimentation of *Sgt. Pepper* and beyond.

The end of this late middle period coincided with the band's final 31-date world tour between June and August 1966. They would perform only three songs from *Help!* and *Rubber Soul* ('Yesterday', 'Nowhere Man' and 'If I Needed Someone') and precisely none from *Revolver*. Their last fee-paying public performance was at Candlestick Park in San Francisco, the home of the San Francisco Giants, on 29 August 1966.

'Pop music in 1966,' wrote Jon Savage in his insightful *1966: The Year The Decade Exploded* (2015), 'was no longer simple commerce, teen romance or good times, but something else: a total immersive experience, the popular form that, out of all the arts, truly reflected contemporary life.'

They took an extended break from Beatledom that autumn. John flew to Germany to take part in a film called *How I Won The War*. George went to India for five weeks to meet with and learn from Ravi Shankar. Paul went on safari to Kenya (or died in a car crash, depending on who you believe). Ringo stayed at home with one-year-old son Zak after a short trip to see John in Spain, where film production had moved in mid-October.

The Beatles jointly returned to EMI on 24 November 1966. It was five months since they had finished 'She Said She Said'. Their aim: to record an album to be called *Sgt. Pepper's Lonely Hearts Club Band*, starting with a new song of John's, which he had written in Spain, called 'Strawberry Fields Forever'.

As David Quantick said in *Q* in 2000, 'There's a case to be made that the Beatles went on to do *Sgt. Pepper* because there was nowhere else to go but too far. With *Revolver*, they had mapped out the pop universe so perfectly that all they could do next was tear it up and start again.'

... to be continued ...

Bibliography

Babiuk, A., *Beatles Gear* (Backbeat, San Francisco, 2002).

Badman, K., *The Beatles After The Break-Up 1970-2000* (Omnibus Press, London, 1993).

Beatles, The, *The Complete Beatles Scores* (Hal Leonard, Wisconsin, 2000).

Beatles, The, *The Beatles Anthology* (Cassel & Co, London, 2000).

Bramwell, T. and Kingsland, R., *Magical Mystery Tours* (St. Martin's Press, New York, 2005).

Braun, M., *'Love Me Do' The Beatles' Progress* (Penguin, London, 1994).

Brown, P. & Gaines, S., *All You Need Is Love: The Beatles In Their Own Words* (St. Martins, London, 2024).

Carrera, M., The Beatles *Let It Be* 50th Deluxe Box Set – What's New? (unpublished notes).

Clayson, A. & Sutcliffe, P., *Stuart Sutcliffe: The Lost Beatle* (Pan, London, 1994).

Coleman, R., *Brian Epstein* (Penguin, London, 1990).

Davies, H., *The Beatles: The Authorised Biography* (Heinemann, London, 1968).

Davies, H., *The Quarrymen* (Omnibus Press, London, 2001).

Egan, S. [ed], *The Mammoth Book Of The Beatles* (Constable & Robinson, London, 2009).

Emerick, G. and Massey, H., *Here There And Everywhere: My Life Recording The Music Of The Beatles* (Gotham Books, New York, 2007).

Englehardt, K., *Beatles Undercover* (Collector's Guide Publishing, Burlington, 1998)

Everett, W., *The Beatles As Musicians: Revolver Through The Anthology* (Oxford University Press, Oxford, 1999).

Everett, W., *The Beatles As Musicians: The Quarry Men Through Rubber Soul* (Oxford University Press, Oxford, 2001).

Frame, P., *The Beatles And Some Other Guys* (Omnibus Press, London, 1997).

Goldman, A., *The Lives Of John Lennon* (Bantam, London, 1988).

Gould, J., *Can't Buy Me Love: The Beatles, Britain And America* (Piatkus, London, 2007).

Hammack, J., *The Beatles Recording Reference Manual: Volume 1: My Bonnie Through Beatles For Sale (1961-1964)* (CreateSpace, 2017).

Hammack, J., *The Beatles Recording Reference Manual: Volume 2: Help! Through Revolver (1965-1966)* (CreateSpace, 2018).

Hammack, J., *The Beatles Recording Reference Manual: Volume 3: Sgt. Pepper's Lonely Hearts Club Band Through Magical Mystery Tour (Late 1966-1967)* (CreateSpace, 2018).

Hammack, J., *The Beatles Recording Reference Manual: Volume 4: The Beatles Through Yellow Submarine (Late 1966-1967)* (CreateSpace, 2019).

Hammack, J., *The Beatles Recording Reference Manual: Volume 5: Let It Be Through Abbey Road (1969-1970)* (CreateSpace, 2020).

Harrison, G., *I Me Mine* (Weidenfeld & Nicholson, London, 2002).

Harry, B., *The Encyclopaedia Of Beatles People* (Blandford, London, 1997).

Hertsgaard, M., *A Day In The Life – The Music And Artistry Of The Beatles* (Delacorte Press, New York, 1995).

Herzogenrath, W. and Hansen, D., *John Lennon Drawings Performances Films* (Thames and Hudson, London, 1995).

Lewisohn, M., *The Beatles Recording Sessions* (Hamlyn, London, 1988).

Lewisohn, M., *The Complete Beatles Chronicle* (Pyramid Books, London, 1992).

Lewisohn, M., *All These Years: Volume 1 'Tune In' [Extended Version]* (Little Brown, London, 2013).

McCartney, P., *Blackbird Singing – Poems And Lyrics 1965-1999* (Faber and Faber, London, 2001).

McCartney, P., *The Lyrics: 1956 To The Present* (Penguin, London, 2021).

MacDonald, I., *Revolution In The Head – The Beatles' Records And The Sixties* (Pimlico, London, 1998).

Madinger, C. and Easter, M., *Eight Arms To Hold You* (44. 1 Productions Inc., USA, 2001).

Martin, G. and Pearson, W., *Summer Of Love: The Making Of Sgt. Pepper* (Macmillan, London, 1994).

Miles, B., *Many Years From Now* (Secker & Warburg, London, 1997).

Norman, P., *Shout!* (Corgi, London, 1981).

O'Donnell, J., *The Day John Met Paul* (Penguin, London, 1996).

Peebles, A., *The Lennon Tapes* (BBC, London, 1981).

Pedler, D., *The Songwriting Secrets Of The Beatles* (Omnibus Press, London, 2003/2017).

Philo, S., *British Invasion: The Crosscurrents Of Musical Influence* (Tempo, Lanham, 2014).

Riley, T., *Tell Me Why – A Beatles Commentary* (Vintage, New York, 1988).

Riley, T., *Lennon – The Man, The Myth, The Music* (Hyperion, New York, 2011).

Rodriguez, R., *Revolver: How The Beatles Re-Imagined Rock 'N' Roll* (Backbeat, Milwaukee, 2012).

Savage, J., *1966: The Year The Decade Exploded* (Faber & Faber, London, 2015).

Spignesi, S., *The Beatles Book Of Lists* (Citadel, Secaucus, 1998).

Spizer, B., *The Beatles Records On Vee-Jay* (498, New Orleans, 1998).

Spizer, B., *The Beatles Story On Capitol Records – Part One: Beatlemania & The Singles* (498, New Orleans, 2000).

Spizer, B., *The Beatles Story On Capitol Records – Part Two: The Albums* (498, New Orleans, 2000).

Sulpy, D. and Schweighardt, R., *Get Back – The Beatles' Let It Be Disaster [Drugs, Divorce And A Slipping Image]* (Helter Skelter, London, 1998).

Sulpy, D., *The 910's Guide To The Beatles' Outtakes [3rd Edition]* (Poptomes, Jackson, 1999).

Sulpy, D., *The 910's Guide To The Beatles' Outtakes: Part One [4th Edition]* (The 910, Jackson, 2001).

Sulpy, D., *The 910's Guide To The Beatles' Outtakes: Part Two – The Complete Get Back Sessions* (The 910, Jackson, 2001).

Sulpy, D., *The 910's Guide To The Beatles' Outtakes: Part Three – The Core Collection* (The 910, Jackson, 2002)

Sulpy, D., *The 910's Guide To The Beatles' Outtakes 2004 Edition* (The 910, Jackson, 2004)

Weiner, A. J., *The Beatles: The Ultimate Recording Guide* (Facts on File, New York, 1992)

Wenner, J., *Lennon Remembers* (Penguin, Harmondsworth, 1973).

Williams, A. and Marshall, W., *The Man Who Gave The Beatles Away* (Coronet, London, 1976).

Winn, J., *Lifting Latches: The Beatles' Recorded Legacy, Volume Three, Inside The Beatles Vaults* (Multiplus Books, Sharon VT, 2005).

Winn, J., *Way Beyond Compare: The Beatles' Recorded Legacy, Volume One, 1957-1965* (Three Rivers Press, New York, 2008).

Winn, J., *That Magic Feeling: The Beatles' Recorded Legacy, Volume Two, 1966-1970* (Three Rivers Press, New York, 2009).

Womack, K., *Maximum Volume: The Life Of Beatles Producer George Martin The Early Years 1926-1966* (Orphans Publishing, Leominster, 2017).

Womack, K., *Sound Pictures: The Life Of Beatles Producer George Martin The Later Years 1966-2016* (Orphans Publishing, Leominster, 2018).

Would you like to write for Sonicbond Publishing?

At Sonicbond Publishing we are always on the look-out for authors, particularly for our two main series:

On Track. Mixing fact with in depth analysis, the On Track series examines the work of a particular musical artist or group. All genres are considered from easy listening and jazz to 60s soul to 90s pop, via rock and metal.

On Screen. This series looks at the world of film and television. Subjects considered include directors, actors and writers, as well as entire television and film series. As with the On Track series, we balance fact with analysis.

While professional writing experience would, of course, be an advantage the most important qualification is to have real enthusiasm and knowledge of your subject. First-time authors are welcomed, but the ability to write well in English is essential.

Sonicbond Publishing has distribution throughout Europe and North America, and all books are also published in E-book form. Authors will be paid a royalty based on sales of their book.

Further details are available from www.sonicbondpublishing.co.uk. To contact us, complete the contact form there or email info@sonicbondpublishing.co.uk